Listen, Talk, Communicate

David Self

Macmillan Education

First published 1987

Published by MACMILLAN EDUCATION LTD
Houndmills, Basingstoke, Hampshire RG21 2XS
and London
Companies and representatives
throughout the world

Designed by Linda Reed

Phototypeset in Optima and Baskerville by
Styleset Limited, Warminster, Wiltshire

Printed in Great Britain by
Camelot Press, Southampton

British Library Cataloguing in Publication Data
Self, David
Listen, talk, communicate.—(Developing
language skills. Speech; 1)
1. English language—Spoken English
I. Title II. Series
428.3   PE1135

ISBN 0-333-42761-0

Contents

Acknowledgements

The author and publishers wish to acknowledge the following photograph sources: Anglia TV, page 41; BBC Enterprise, pages 1, 117; Jim Brownbill, pages 5, 6 top, 97; Camera Press, page 6 bottom left, 47; J. Allan Cash Ltd, page 100; Colorsport, page 53; Cow & Gate Ltd, page 65; Sally and Richard Greenhill, page 131; Andrew Harrison, page 39; Rodney Jennings, page 106; McNaught Syndicate, page 10; Thames Television, page 113; United Artists, page 18; Michael Wilcox, page 6 bottom right. The author and publishers wish to thank the following who have kindly given permission for the use of copyright material: John Arlott for extracts from an interview and a radio commentary; Associated Book Publishers (UK) Ltd for an extract from *Clockwise* by Michael Frayn, Methuen, 'The Black and White' from *A Slight Ache and Other Plays* by Harold Pinter and a poem from *Knots* by R. D. Laing, Tavistock Publications; Blackstaff Press Ltd for an extract from 'The Miraculous Candidate' from *Secrets and Other Stories* by Bernard MacLaverty; British Broadcasting Corporation for extracts by Colin Smith from *Help Yourself: Are You Speaking Proper* and an extract spoken by Brian Redhead from *Help with Spoken English*; Carcanet Press Ltd for 'The First Man of Mercury' from *Poems of Thirty Years* by Edwin Morgan; Century Hutchinson Ltd for extracts from *The Penny World* by Arthur Barton, Hutchinson; Comedia for extracts from *Open the Box* by Jane Root; Gerald Duckworth & Co Ltd for six short stories from *It's True . . . It Happened to a Friend* by Rodney Dale; Victor Gollancz Ltd for an extract from *The Final Test* by Gareth Owen; the *Guardian* for 'Chatterbox charter' by Wendy Berliner, 13.12.79; Harcourt Brace Jovanovich, Inc. for 'Elephants are Different to Different People' from *The Complete Poems of Carl Sandburg*. Copyright © 1950 by Carl Sandburg, renewed 1978 by Margaret Sandburg, Helga Sandburg Crile and Janet Sandburg; David Higham Associates Ltd on behalf of Keith Waterhouse for an extract from 'Call of the Wild' from *Mondays, Thursdays*, Michael Joseph Ltd; Hodder & Stoughton Ltd for an extract from 'Nathan's True Self' by Alison Price from *Cold Feet* ed. Jean Richards; Michael Joseph Ltd for extracts from *A Kestrel for a Knave* by Barry Hines © Barry Hines; Edward Kelsey for an extract from *The Art of Conversation*; Macmillan Company of Australia Pty Ltd for an extract from *The Spoken Word* by Richard McRoberts; Julia MacRae Books for an extract from *Bloxworth Blue* by William Corlett; Peter O'Sullevan for an extract from a radio commentary; Oxford University Press for an extract from *Brother in the Land* by Robert Swindells; John Percival for extracts from 'The Hounding of the Hunters', the *Listener*, 18.3.82; *Psychology Today* for an extract from the April issue, 1976; Python Productions Ltd for 'The Parrot Sketch' by Graham Chapman and John Cleese; Jennifer Rogers and Bernard Lovell for an extract from *Adults in Education*, BBC Publications; Watson, Little Limited on behalf of Myra Schneider for an extract from *If Only I Could Walk*, William Heinemann Ltd; A. P. Watt Ltd on behalf of Fritz Spiegl for an extract from the *Listener*, 12.12.85.

Every effort has been made to trace all the copyright holders but if any have been inadvertently overlooked the publishers will be pleased to make the necessary arrangement at the first opportunity.

Preface

By the time you reach secondary school, most of you have been talking reasonably well for seven or eight years. So who needs lessons in how to talk? Don't we do it all of the time? (Too much of the time, some might say.)

We shall come back to those questions (and their answers) at the end of Chapter 1. At this point, let us just note that this is a book for everyone who wants to be able to talk confidently and effectively. It is not a book that is secretly trying to change the sort of person you are by making you 'talk posh' – nor for that matter is it trying to making everyone speak 'common'. I do believe however that there are effective and ineffective ways of talking and that what is right for one occasion may not be best on another.

The book is also based on the belief that we all need to talk for two main purposes. The first is to sort out our own ideas. Most of us don't know what we think about any given topic until we say it out loud. Talking gives us a chance to sort out our ideas.

The second purpose in talking is of course to communicate with other people – without boring them! We need, we *want*, to be able to share ideas, news and gossip with other people. We need to be able to explain things and to find things out, efficiently and without embarrassment.

Because oral communication is a two-way process, just as important (more important, perhaps) is listening. The good communicator is, first of all, a good listener. So that is why the title of this book is *Listen, Talk, Communicate*.

Its sequel is *Listen, Talk, Evaluate* which leads on to those particular skills you must possess (and perhaps demonstrate) if you are to gain a 'pass' grade in Oral Communication (without which you cannot pass GCSE English).

There is also a Teacher's Book which contains additional material which may be photocopied for use in certain exercises (to save you having to write in this book).

Additionally, there is a set of tapes, *Help With Spoken English*. These are recordings of four radio programmes, broadcast by BBC Education on Radio 4 for Schools in the series *GCSE English*. Although book and tapes can be used independently of each other, the tapes contain material which supplements and illustrates many of the topics covered by this book and its companion. More details of these can be found in the Teacher's Book.

1 Without talking...

You may not have too much difficulty in remembering a time when you were told to get on with some work 'without talking'. You may also be able to remember a time when you have been in trouble for talking when you should have been quiet.

But there are some people who keep quiet when they should be talking.

The broadcaster Brian Redhead recalls this occasion:

I once interviewed a man who never said anything. He was a professor of an American university....

We'd arranged the interview. I'd explained what I'd ask him. Five areas or topics seemed interesting. He nodded wisely. We went in the studio. I asked the first question.

Nothing happened. He opened his mouth. The perspiration ran down his forehead like Niagara – and he didn't say anything.

I waited for what seemed like three hours but was probably five seconds. I answered the question. I asked the second one and thought this bloke's never going to say a word. I answered the second question, rolled merrily through the third, fourth and fifth and said, 'Professor, thank you very much.'

A picture tells a story

We don't always need to talk to tell each other things. It was just the look of the American professor that made Brian Redhead decide he was never going to say anything.

Pictures can also tell us things. For example, they can give us information or directions – without using words.

■ These 'pictograms' can all be found on British Rail stations. Working in pairs, discuss what each one must indicate. Write down your answers.

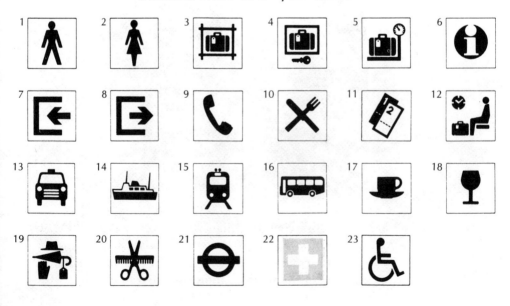

Screenplay

Just as a pictogram can give information or directions without words, so a film can tell a story without words (or 'dialogue'). Indeed some films have very little dialogue, yet we have no trouble in understanding them.

The following excerpt comes from the screenplay (or script) of the film *Clockwise*. In it, John Cleese plays a character called Stimpson, the headmaster of a large comprehensive school. Stimpson has a public-address (PA) system by which he can speak to the whole school. 'Nine-twenty' is the time each morning that he sees 'wrong-doers'.

from: Clockwise

[The playground of a mixed comprehensive school housed in modern buildings. It is just before the start of morning school in late September, and the playground is crowded.

Various shots of pupils messing around, playing, chatting, jeering at each other, etc. Pan up to:

Window of Headmaster's study. The neat regular lines of the window fill the frame, like the digital display of the alarm clock in Scene 1. One of the windows is open, and Stimpson can be seen inside, visibly watching the scene in the playground. Suddenly he picks up a pair of binoculars and looks through them.

Cut to a group of boys in the playground. Two boys are just beginning to torture a third. A fourth boy, one of the persecutors, glances upwards in the direction of the headmaster's study. It is evidently a habitual precaution. What he sees makes him shake the arms of the torturers. They glance up in their turn, and let their victim go. He glances up no less guiltily. Cut to:

Window of Headmaster's study. Stimpson lowers the binoculars, satisfied. Then he puts them to his eyes again, looking in a different direction. He picks up a microphone.]

STIMPSON *[his voice hugely magnified by PA]* Right – Orridge, Popple, Patel.

[Cut to Orridge, Popple Patel. The first two are looking at a school atlas that Patel is holding, in the most law-abiding and studious way. They look up, surprised to be addressed in their innocence.

3

The noise in the playground dies down.]

STIMPSON *[out of view, over PA]* Nine-twenty.

[Patel puts a hand to his chest to mean, What – us? Me? As he does so a number of photographs slide out from behind the atlas. He retrieves them quickly, glancing up in the direction of the headmaster's study.]

MICHAEL FRAYN

■ Discuss what we are told by the pictures we see on the screen. For example, what does the first shot tell us? Location? Time of day?

■ How could the film tell us it was late September?

■ What do we learn about Stimpson from this sequence? What sort of man is he? Can you list any of his likes and dislikes?

■ Even if we do not see Patel's photographs in close-up, what does his final glance tell us?

The birds and the bees

Do you believe that animals, birds and insects can 'talk' to each other?
☐ Do birds sing to each other?
☐ Do bees communicate with one another?
☐ Do horses talk to each other?
☐ Do dogs have a language?
☐ Do apes and monkeys have their own languages?

■ How far can your group or class answer these questions for yourselves?

■ Who could you ask to help you to answer them?

■ With their help, try to answer the five questions.

Body language

Human beings, as well as animals, pass information or messages one to another without using words. For example, the way a person looks can tell you what mood he or she is in.

We also communicate by using gestures...

...and by the way we sit or stand.

This way of communicating is sometimes called 'body language' or 'non-verbal communication'.

■ Working in pairs and some distance apart, try to convey the following messages to your partner without using any words or sounds. Don't work through the list in order: your partner has to guess (and write down in order) the messages you are conveying.

☐ 'Will you please hurry up?'
☐ 'Shut the door quietly and come and sit by me.'
☐ 'Look, I'm the boss and don't you forget it.'
☐ 'I'm not interested. Push off.'
☐ 'What on earth am I doing getting involved in this?'
☐ 'Don't I look good!'
☐ 'Haven't I done well!'
☐ 'Take it or leave it: I couldn't care less.'
☐ 'He's crazy.'
☐ 'I'm not taking any notice of anyone.'

■ Now work in groups of three or four and try to convey the following messages using only your head and face. See who can convey each message most clearly and yet without being too obvious.

☐ 'What an idiot he/she is!'
☐ 'Wowee! He/she looks all right!'
☐ 'You're in real trouble, aren't you?'
☐ 'Hi!'
☐ 'Everything's fine.'
☐ 'Sorry.'
☐ 'Go on, please.'
☐ 'Really? That's interesting.'
☐ 'I don't believe you.'
☐ 'I didn't hear what you said.'

Note that 'body language' can vary from culture to culture. An American businessman may think it friendly and 'right' to stare a new acquaintance straight in the eye; an Asian may think that lowering the eyes and looking downwards is a sign of respect to a person.

People-watching

It is said that in any conversation over half the 'messages' or communications from one person to another are non-verbal. Become a secret people-watcher and discover if this is true!

■ Do you believe body language can be misleading and can be used to hide your true thoughts? Do you think this boy could be right?

Nodding his head in an understanding manner
Thinking he knows me,
The vain, conceited thoughts of the teacher who
Believes that from my outward actions
He can tell what goes on in the inner recesses of my mind.
He is wrong:
He does not know that some of my actions are assumed
To please him, to make him trust me.
I am not what he may think:
Who I am, only I know.

JONATHAN BAILLIE

Banana gun

■ In pairs, rehearse this mime so that you can present it using only body language to make each point.

A enters timidly and cautiously, looking around to see that nobody else is around. Very slowly and with great care, A takes a banana from a pocket. It is obviously very precious. A is on the point of peeling it but gradually begins to be aware that there is still nobody else around. A gains in self-confidence. At first self-consciously but gradually with increasing enjoyment, A begins to play at using it as a revolver, pretending to fire at imaginary victims. By now, A is confident and proud.

After some time, A tires of the game and eats the banana with some dignity and quiet pleasure. Once it is finished, A takes a second banana from a pocket and begins to play the same imaginary game but this time more slowly and seriously.

At this point B approaches from behind A and unseen by A. B communicates to us that A is, sadly, mad but also harmless: it is all a great pity and nothing can be done about it.

After a short while, A senses someone else is present. For a moment, A seems to lose all confidence and to be overcome with embarrassment. Then, with a change of mind and with all the confidence in the world, A turns slowly on B and fires. A gunshot is heard and B collapses to the ground, in silent agony, mortally wounded.

A shows a complete lack of concern and leaves with great dignity, eating the second banana.

■ Invent and develop your own mimed stories, using gestures and facial expressions to communicate the plot and characters' feelings.

Ers and ums

As well as body talk, there is another way we communicate without using words. Most of us make *vocal* sounds (that is, sounds made by the voice) which are not proper words. For example, some people say 'er' or 'um' a lot when they are not sure of what they are talking about.

■ How do you think the following 'non-words' sound? What different meanings could each one have?
□ Mm.
□ Uh.
□ Uh?
□ Ah.
□ Ahh!
□ Huh.

■ What other 'non-words' do you use a lot? How might they be spelt?

Some 'non-words' can have many meanings:

Gibberish

Try inventing a gibberish language, perhaps using just one main syllable: 'Dob er dob. Dob. Dob dob dobbity *dob* do-dob dob... Dob?'

■ Working in pairs and using your own gibberish sounds, create one or more of the following conversations:
□ Two teachers in a staff room or common room talk about the classes they have taught that morning.
□ Two friends discover a corpse and are unsure whether it is dead or what they should do.
□ One partner discovers that the other is sad and sets about cheering him or her up – successfully. They decide to celebrate.
□ One partner tells the other off for breaking something fairly valuable. The offender at first resents being told off but then changes and accepts all the blame and guilt – so much so that this makes the first person guilty and apologetic in turn.

■ In groups of four:
□ Three speak gibberish and do not understand English. The fourth speaks only English and not gibberish. This person is lost in a strange town, has forgotten the name of the hotel in which he or she is staying but remembers what it is near (make up your mind as to what). Can he or she discover how to get there? (Try repeating the exercise with three English speakers and a 'lost' gibberish speaker.)

■ How successful are you and your partner at communicating one of these conversations (or another of your own invention) to another pair (or larger group)?

Why talk?

Obviously we can communicate without using words. Equally obviously, without words, without *language*, we are limited in what we can communicate. (You have probably already tried exercises in this book which have not worked.) But do we have to *learn* to talk? Certainly a baby has to – but do people of your age need to?

To get on with different people in different situations, it *is* necessary to go on learning and finding different ways of talking. We need to be able to talk easily and confidently in order to share experiences and emotions with friends and those we care for. We also need to be able to talk (and *listen*) effectively in order to gain information, jobs, new ideas, help and comfort. Not to have the courage to ask a question at a political, union or club meeting or at an interview is to have a kind of handicap. Not to be able to talk effectively and appropriately and not to be a good listener is also to be restricted. What is more, we have to gain a sort of oral fluency in our mother tongue before we can start to develop any fluency in the written language; and most of us, throughout our lives, will use the spoken far more than the written language.

Even so it is still often necessary to defend setting aside part of the school timetable for oral work. The commoner arguments or attitudes that are advanced against devoting time to it (particularly in English lessons) are:
  - 'Everyone is able to talk so there's no need to teach them how.'
  - 'They learn to speak in the home – there's no need to duplicate the process at school.'
  - 'If they're talking they can't be learning. All talk means no "do".' (This attitude may spring from

the disciplinary point: talking in class is 'naughty'.)
- 'Talk happens in all the lessons anyway; there's no need to make an extra special thing of it in English.'
- 'It is just for the exhibitionist. It favours the child with the gift of the gab and is unfair on the shy or withdrawn child.'
- 'Oral work means lower standards than written work because it'll take up valuable teaching time. It's anti-intellectual.'

Two more arguments are put forward against oral work in the secondary school:
- 'They should have achieved oral fluency in the primary school.'
- 'Adolescents don't want to talk. They're naturally shy or silent.'

■ What do you think are the reasons that some people make such remarks? How would you answer them?
■ With which of the two ideas below do you agree?

Chatterbox charter

By Wendy Berliner, Education Staff

A GROUP of English teachers from seven Avon comprehensive schools claim that chatter in the classroom is an effective way for children to learn. In a working paper published today by the Schools Council, the teachers say they want to break down the belief that talking in class is time-wasting.

They claim that talking has a place with reading and writing as an effective way of educating. Cases of pupils being better able to understand literature after they had been allowed to talk about it among themselves are described in detail.

from *The Guardian*, 13.12.79

Silence is golden

IN WHAT appears to be a last, despairing effort to teach its pupils decent grammar, a Chicago school has abolished talking altogether in some classrooms and instituted a system whereby the children can only communicate with each other and with their teachers by memorandum. Each pupil is provided with a pigeonhole from which he or she receives the teacher's instructions and any communications from fellow pupils. All memos are collected at the end of the day and the grammar corrected. After the first nine weeks the two parts of the school have been tested on their grammar with resounding victory for the memo classes who made only one third of the mistakes compared with the remainder of the school.

from *The Sunday Times*, 4.4.76, quoting *Psychology Today*, US Edition, April issue.

Developing spoken language skills

This book and its sequel have been planned and written to help anyone who wants to feel not only confident and competent as a talker (and listener) but also an expert! In particular, the two books have been devised to help GCSE candidates who, of course, must gain at least Grade 5 in Oral Communication (which includes both talking and listening) in order to gain a grade in the whole subject of English. Your teacher will be keeping a record of your achievements. It will probably help you if you keep your own record as well and your teacher may be able to give you a copy of a form (from the Teacher's Book that accompanies these two books) on which you can record your own progress and achievements.

2 You see, what happened was...

□ Are you sometimes stuck for words?
□ When asked a question in class, are you often unsure what to say?
□ Do you tend to say 'Er...' and 'Um...' a lot?
□ Do you find it hard to say what you mean?
□ Are you bothered if you have to speak to the whole class or a large group of people?
□ Do you have problems on the phone?
□ Are you embarrassed by the sound of your voice on tape?
□ Do you dread having to speak in public?

You are not alone! In a survey, 30 000 Americans were asked what they feared most. 41 per cent answered, 'Having to speak to a group of people'.

So what's the problem?

What don't you like doing and what don't you mind doing?

■ Make a copy of these tables and tick the box that shows what you feel about each of the following:

	Don't like doing	Don't mind doing	Quite like doing
At school Answering questions in class			
Joining in group discussions			
Discussing work with a teacher			
Having to say what you think about something			
Giving a talk in front of the class			

14

	Don't like doing	Don't mind doing	Quite like doing
Out of school Having to give directions			
Joining in conversations with friends			
Phoning a stranger			
Being given instructions you've got to remember			
Being interviewed			

So that's the problem. By the time you have worked through this book, you should be wanting to come back to this table and remove any ticks from the left-hand column and replace them in the central or right-hand columns!

Something to say

All of us have far more to say than we sometimes think. If you have read the novel *A Kestrel for a Knave*, you will perhaps remember this English lesson.

from: A Kestrel for a Knave (Kes)

'Right 4C. To continue. Fact.'

He swung one arm and indicated the board behind him. On it was printed:

FACT AND FICTION

'What did we say fact was, Armitage?'

'Something that's happened, Sir.'

'Right. Something that has happened. Something that we know is real. The things that we read about in newspapers, or hear on the news. Events, accidents, meetings; the things that we see with our own eyes, the things all about us; all these are facts. Have you got that? Is that clear?'

Chorus: 'Yes, Sir.'

'Right then. Now if I asked Anderson for some facts about himself, what could he tell us?'

'Sir! Sir!'

'All right! All right! Just put your hands up. There's no need to jump down my throat. Jordan?'

'He's wearing jeans.'

'Good. Mitchell?'

'He's got black hair.'

'Yes. Fisher?'

'He lives down Shallowbank Crescent.'

'Do you, Anderson?'

'Yes, Sir.'

'Right then. Now all these facts are about Anderson, but they're not particularly interesting facts. Perhaps Anderson can tell us something about himself that *is* interesting. A really interesting fact.'

There was a massive 'Woooo!' from the rest of the class. Mr Farthing grinned and rode it; then he raised his hands to control it.

'Quietly now. Quietly.'

The class quietened, still grinning. Anderson stared at his desk, blushing.

'I don't know owt, Sir.'

'Anything at all, Anderson, anything that's happened to you, or that you've seen which sticks in your mind.'

'I can't think of owt, Sir.'

'What about when you were little? It doesn't have to be fantastic, just something that you've remembered.'

Anderson began to smile and looked up.

'There's summat. It's nowt though.'

'It must be if you remember it.'

'It's daft really.'

'Well tell us then, and let's all have a laugh.'

'Well it was once when I was a kid. I was at Junior School, I think, or somewhere like that, and went down to Fowlers Pond, me and this other kid. Reggie Clay they called him, he didn't come to this school; he flitted and went away somewhere. Anyway it was Spring, tadpole time, and it's swarming with tadpoles down there in Spring. Edges of t'pond are all black with 'em, and me and this other kid started to catch 'em. It was easy, all you did, you just put your hands together and scooped a handful of water up and you'd got a handful of tadpoles. Anyway we were mucking about with 'em, picking 'em up and chucking 'em back and things, and we were on about taking some home, but we'd no jam jars. So this kid, Reggie, says, "Take thi wellingtons off and put some in there, they'll be all right 'til tha gets home." So I took 'em off and we put some water in 'em and then we started to put taddies in 'em. We kept ladling 'em in and I says to this kid, "Let's have a competition, thee have one welli' and I'll have t'other, and we'll see who can get most in!" So he started to fill one welli' and I started to fill t'other. We must have been at it hours, and they got thicker and thicker, until at t'end there was no water left in 'em, they were just jam packed wi'taddies.

'You ought to have seen 'em, all black and shiny, right up to t'top. When we'd finished we kept digging us fingers into 'em and whipping 'em up at each other, all shouting and excited like. Then this kid says to me, "I bet tha daren't put one on." And I says, "I bet tha daren't." So we said we'd put one on each. We wouldn't though, we kept reckoning to, then running away, so we tossed up and who lost had to do it first. And I lost, oh, and you'd to take your socks off an' all. So I took my socks off, and I kept looking at this welli' full of taddies, and this kid kept saying, "Go on then, tha' frightened, tha' frightened." I was an' all. Anyway I shut my eyes and started to put my foot in. Oooo. It was just like putting your feet into live jelly. They were frozen. And when my foot went down, they all came over t'top of my wellington, and when I got my foot to t'bottom, I could feel 'em squashing about between my toes.

'Anyway I'd done it, and I says to this kid, "Thee put thine on now." But he wouldn't, he was dead scared, so I put it on instead. I'd got used to it then, it was all right after a bit; it sent your legs all excited and tingling like. When I'd got 'em both on I started to walk up to this kid, waving my arms and making spook noises; and as I walked they all came squelching over t'tops again and ran down t'sides. This kid look frightened to death, he kept looking down at my wellies so I tried to run at him and they all spurted up my legs. You ought to have seen him. He just screamed out and ran home roaring.

'It was a funny feeling though when he'd gone; all quiet, with nobody there, and up to t'knees in tadpoles.'

Silence. The class up to their knees in tadpoles.

BARRY HINES

'Talk' does not always come so easily. Later, in the same lesson, the English teacher (Mr Farthing) tries to get another boy (Billy Casper) to tell a similar story from *his* experience. Billy is shyer than Anderson.

He pivoted round on one foot and thrust an arm out at Billy.

'I'm giving you two minutes to think of something lad, and if you haven't started then, the whole class is coming back at four!'

There was a general stiffening of backs and looking round wide-eyed, accompanied by grumbling and interspersed with eh's and threatening encouragements.

'Come on, Billy.'

''Else tha dies.'

'Say owt.'

'If I've to come back I'll kill him.'

Billy tried to blink back the tears shining in his eyes.

'I'm waiting, Casper.'

Mr Farthing sat down and nudged back his jacket sleeve to look at his watch.

'We haven't got all day, Casper.'

'Tell him about thi hawk, Billy.'

'If anyone else calls out, it will be the last he'll make! . . . What hawk, Casper? . . . Casper, I'm speaking to you.'

Billy continued to show Mr Farthing the top of his head.

'Look this way boy when I'm speaking to you.'

Billy looked up slowly.

'And stop sulking just because somebody says a few words to you! . . . Now then, what's this about this hawk? What is it, a stuffed one?'

The shout of laughter from the class spilled the first tears on to Billy's face, and left Mr Farthing looking about in surprise at these opposing reactions to his question.

'What's funny about that?'

Tibbut half stood up, placing the weight of his body on the desk top as he shot one arm up.

'Well, Tibbut?'

'He's got a hawk, Sir. It's a kestrel. He's mad about it. He never knocks about wi' anybody else now, he just looks after this hawk all t'time. He's crackers wi' it!'

Billy turned on him, the movement releasing a fresh head of tears into wobbly halting motion down his cheeks.

'It's better than thee anyday, Tibby!'

'I told you, Sir, he goes daft if you say owt about it.'

'Right, Casper, sit down.'

Billy sat down and wiped his cheeks on the shoulders of his jacket. Mr Farthing rested his elbows on his desk and tapped his teeth with his thumb nails, waiting for Billy to collect himself.

'Now then, Billy, tell me about this hawk. Where did
you get it from?'

'Found it.'

'Where?'

'In t'wood.'

'What had happened to it? Was it injured or
something?'

'It was a young 'un. It must have tumbled from a
nest.'

'And how long have you had it?'

'Since last year.'

'All that time? Where do you keep it?'

'In a shed.'

'And what do you feed it on?'

'Beef. Mice. Birds.'

'Isn't it cruel though, keeping it in a shed all the
time? Wouldn't it be happier flying free?'

Billy looked at Mr Farthing for the first time since he
had told him to sit down.

'I don't keep it in t'shed all t'time. I fly it every day.'

'And doesn't it fly away? I thought hawks were wild
birds.'

''Course it don't fly away. I've trained it.'

Billy looked round, as though daring anyone to
challenge this authority.

'Trained it? I thought you'd to be an expert to train
hawks.'

'Well I did it.'

'Was it difficult?'

''Course it was. You've to be right . . . right patient wi'
'em and take your time.'

'Well tell me how you did it then. I've never met a
falconer before, I suppose I must be in select company.'

Billy hutched his chair up and leaned forward over
his desk.

'Well what you do is, you train 'em through their
stomachs. You can only do owt wi' 'em when they're
hungry, so you do all your training at feeding time.

'I started training Kes after I'd had her about a
fortnight, when she was hard penned, that means her
tail feathers and wing feathers had gone hard at their
bases. You have to use a torch at night and keep

20

inspecting 'em. It's easy if you're quiet, you just go up to her as she's roosting, and spread her tail and wings. If t'feathers are blue near t'bottom o' t'shaft, that means there's blood in 'em an' they're still soft, so they're not ready yet. When they're white and hard then they're ready, an' you can start training her then.

'Kes wa' as fat as a pig though at first. All young hawks are when you first start to train 'em, and you can't do much wi' 'em 'til you've got their weight down. You've to be ever so careful though, you don't just starve 'em, you weigh 'em before every meal and gradually cut their food down, 'til you go in one time an' she's keen, an' that's when you start getting somewhere.'

BARRY HINES

Despite his early fear, Casper *has* something interesting to share. He catches the interest of the whole class – and surprises Mr Farthing.

Remember: all of us have far more to say than we sometimes think.

■ Suppose someone you know (who is not keen on talking in public) is in that English set. Next lesson, it will be his or her turn to tell the group about something interesting that he or she has done.

In a list, write down as many hints as you can think of which will help and encourage him or her to talk easily. (Look back at the two passages: what started Anderson and Casper talking more easily?)

From experience

It is of course easiest to talk about what we know best, about things that have happened to us. Even then it can take some courage – especially as we may not be keen to admit some things.

Obviously everyone wishes to keep some parts of his or her life private but the successful and interesting talker (or 'conversationalist') will often be the one who has the courage to be honest (as Anderson was in talking about the tadpole incident).

■ In groups of four, read aloud the following transcript of what four girls said when talking about their experiences of part-time work. (Have two or three attempts at reading the passage to see if you can make the words sound like conversation rather than 'written-and read' language.)

GIRL 1   There was a friend at school who stopped working at the newsagent's at Ricketwood where I live so I went to the newsagent's and said 'Have you got a job?', and he said 'yes' so I started working there, and I really enjoyed it because I met a lot of people and got on with the people I work for – the money's also good and I enjoy filling up shelves and serving the customers.

GIRL 2   I started work in a newsagent's shop because a friend worked there and she told me she was going to leave so I got my name down there before anybody else. I've left since then but when I worked there it was really good because we had to do stock-taking and it was really interesting and we had to stock up shelves and price things and phone up different companies about new sweets and things they were bringing out. I liked the variation of the job.

GIRL 3   I used to work on an ice-cream van and it was really awful. On the first day – the Saturday, I was up the market and I was finding it very difficult because the ice-cream was very hard and I had to learn how to scoop out these cones and stick them in and I kept breaking the cornettos. People kept saying to me 'Well never mind, dear, try again.' I think I must have wasted about £10 of ice-cream. It was really embarrassing – the boss came along and he said – 'Have you got the idea yet?' I looked at him and said 'No.'

GIRL 4   I was looking for a job and I had no idea what I wanted to do. I needed the money – at that age I was going out and I tried everywhere but a supermarket because I used to think, 'Oh no – not a supermarket.' It was a last resort. I went along to Tesco's and the only thing they asked for was that I was 15 and 3 months. Fine – if that was all they wanted I'd take the job. I was trained for two weekends and that was it. I was put onto a till and I just had to use the till.

GIRL 3   When I was on the van I used to be stuck outside this great big park and this man would come along and he had about 30 children with him. They all wanted cornettos. I mean it's no fun – I didn't have a calculator. I had no pens or pencils, no paper to write on – and those cornettos were about 36p each. I had to add up about 30 of them and then they changed their minds. I was getting really mad.

GIRL 4   The job at the supermarket – I really like the people. I used to go in Saturday morning loving the work. You'd sit at the till and you'd sit 3 hours solid. The customers – on Saturday the market's on – and they'd come in and they're in a bad mood because the market's so crushed. You're a scape-goat for them. They can take their worries out on you. By the mid-afternoon you're sitting and thinking, 'If another customer comes to my till, that's it, I'm going to leave.' And every Saturday I used to leave the shop intending to hand my notice in – and by the next week I'd love the world again. It just carried on like this. It changed my feelings about people altogether.

■ Which girl do you think has been reminded of something that she has done or which has happened to her by what somebody else has said? Who do you think is talking most honestly? And with most courage? Which girl do you find the most interesting speaker? Why?

Group talk: getting organised

☐ At first, most people find it easier to talk in small groups.
☐ It is better if no group is easily distracted by another.

☐ If there are more than five in any group (and
nobody is 'in the chair'), it can end up with two or
more people talking at the same time.
☐ Progress gradually from talking in groups of friends
to talking with people with whom you do not
regularly spend much time in conversation.
☐ Progress from talking about subjects that seem
'easy' or 'safe' to ones (perhaps in the following list
of topics) that require more honesty.

Group talk: intentions

Your group talk or conversation will be more
satisfactory if it has a purpose or intention (decided in
advance). It might be
- enjoyment
- practice in talking on set subjects and so
developing your confidence
- experience in talking to different people
- practice in listening to other people and
responding to their contributions
- recalling your own experiences before reading
another person's account of a similar topic
- recalling your experiences and memories before
writing on a given topic
- exploring a subject before improvising scenes
connected with it
or
- sorting out your ideas before a more formal
discussion group
Remember also that for the oral-communication section
of many examinations, you will have to demonstrate
the skill of participating effectively and appropriately in
small-group conversation.

Topics for talk

The following list is long. It is obviously not suggested
that every group works through the whole list. Some
topics will not be relevant in particular circumstances.

However it is intended to provide plenty of ideas and starting points for small-group 'talk' which can be drawn upon on various and recurring occasions and for a variety of 'intentions'.

The more practice we have in talking with a purpose, the more confident and more fluent we become; and, as we listen to other people's contributions, the better listeners we become.

Talk on these topics will also provide starting points for written work and for improvisation and discussion (see Chapters 5 and 9).

1 *Adults*

Describe a time when you have been very conscious of being a child among adults – perhaps when you have been taken into a room where a lot of adults were drinking; or it might be an occasion when you couldn't understand any of the conversation around you. Try to describe both what was happening and your reactions to it all.

2 *Bullying*

Can you tell of a time when you have been a bully? And of when you have been bullied? Or of when you have watched bullying going on, without joining in?

Can you remember a time when bullying got out of hand and something really serious happened?

Have you ever joined in some bullying and then regretted it? Describe how your attitude altered.

3 *Buying and selling*

Can you describe your experiences of selling anything? Perhaps by an advertisement in a paper? Have you ever sold anything you weren't meant to sell? Have you ever worked in a shop? Have you ever replied to an advertisement in a newspaper or magazine? Or have you ever been talked into buying something you didn't want? Retell any problems (or pleasures) you have experienced while buying or selling things.

4 *Childhood*

What are your earliest memories? Your happiest ones? How do your younger brothers and sisters play? What toys interest them most? What games do you regret having grown out of? Have you kept any toys or dolls or animals from your early childhood? Can you describe any game of 'let's pretend' that you used to play?

Have you ever been conscious that your childhood was coming to an end? Can you describe that moment?

5 Competition

Tell of a time when you tried very hard to win a game, or to do well in some other form of competition – perhaps to come high in a form order. Do you enjoy competing? Or does competition depress and overwhelm you? Have you ever been on a team where one person has not tried? Have you ever been such a person? How did other people react?

6 Dares

Have you ever accepted a dare? Talk about such a time. Can you remember persuading someone else to undertake a risk? How did you do it? What happened? Is there any enjoyment in undertaking something risky? Try to describe it. Can you tell of a dare that went wrong and ended in tragedy? Have you ever prevented a silly dare from taking place, or failed in this attempt? Were you unpopular? What made you act as you did?

7 Failure

Describe a time when you failed on something that mattered a lot to you. (An exam? Getting on a team? Doing well in a test or in a game? In music or a play?) Have you ever had to cope with a friend or relative who had 'failed'? What was difficult about this? What did you say? How do your parents, brothers, sisters, react to your failures? Have you ever deliberately failed at something to disappoint another person or to prove something? What were the effects and results?

8 Fear

Can you talk about a time when you have been really afraid? Of a place? a person? a nightmare? a television programme? What fears did you have when you were younger? Are there still any fears you find it difficult to talk about? Can you describe a time when a fear has suddenly (or gradually) subsided? How did you feel afterwards? Do we enjoy being afraid? Why do we watch horror films?

9 *Fights*

Describe a playground fight you have witnessed, or one you have lost. What other kinds of 'fights' go on at school? Verbal ones? Longlasting ones that smoulder and then flare up suddenly? Can you describe a time you have encouraged a fight? Or actually started one between other people? How did you feel? What sort of fighting occurs within a family? Why? Have you ever not enjoyed winning? When?

10 *Friendship*

How do you make friends? Can you describe an unsuccessful attempt to make friends with someone? Have you ever tried to keep a friendship going when it wouldn't work? Can you describe a time when you have presumed on a friend too much, or when you have been taken for granted? Or when you have been 'left out'? What are the problems of having friends who won't mix easily with each other? What are your parents' attitudes to your friends?

11 *Gangs and clubs*

Describe any gang or 'club' you have belonged to. What did you enjoy about it? Who decided who was to be the boss? What sort of person was he or she? Why did everyone stay together? What did they all get out of it? Recall any pleasurable times you have had with the people in your group now. 'Do you remember the time we . . .?' Why was it fun?

12 *Hardship*

Have you ever had to put up with real hardship? In really bad weather? Because you were being punished unfairly? Because you had been boasting that you could go through with something that proved more testing than you imagined? Describe the hardship of boredom. Or of loneliness. (When have you been really lonely? More lonely than you liked to admit at the time?) What other sorts of hardship do people have to put up with?

13 Holidays

Describe part of the best holiday you have ever had. Or part of the worst: the greatest anticlimax of a holiday. How do you relax? What do you enjoy doing with your spare time? How do you waste time?

14 Loneliness

Have you ever enjoyed being lonely? Talk about your best or worst moment of loneliness. Have you ever been lonely in the middle of a crowd of people? Can you describe a person who enjoys being lonely? What is the opposite of loneliness? Have you ever had a lonely holiday? Describe it. Or a lonely party or weekend?

15 Lost

Describe any time you have been lost, or a time anyone in your family has been lost.

16 Money

Have you ever won a lot of money? Or earned a lot of money? What are their respective pleasures? Have you ever saved up for something? What? Describe the frustrations and satisfactions. Can saving be fun? How? What pocket-money do you receive? How do you plan its use? Is it possible to have too much money?

17 Nagging

How do people nag or 'get at' you? At home? At school? What sort of things do you hate being nagged about? Can you think of anything you are now glad you were nagged about? How do you nag other people? Who? Why? Is it good for them, or not? Have you ever felt you were being nagged about something serious and that the nagging was really getting you down? What? Could you be accused of putting too much pressure on someone else?

18 Old people

Describe an unpleasant old person you know. And a pleasant one. Have you ever visited an old folks' home? What struck you most about it? Have you ever had an argument with an old person? Who 'won'? Was that right? Have you ever felt you were responsible for an old person and that you had to protect them in some way? How do you imagine yourself when really old? What do you dread most, and what do you most look forward to?

19 *Parents*
Describe an occasion when you have watched parents (whom you didn't know) who were failing to cope sensibly with their children (e.g. at the seaside or on a day out). What should they have done? How do parents lose touch with their children? Is this anyone's fault? What can parents do accidentally that embarrasses their children? Have you ever felt sorry for your parents? Have you ever been able to help them in an important way?

20 *Punishment*
Have you ever been glad to be punished – glad at being found out and a worry coming to an end in punishment? What punishments have you suffered without deserving them? What sort of punishments do you prefer?

How do *you* 'punish' people? Your parents? People younger than yourself? What sort of effects (good and bad) have different punishments had on you? Have you ever noticed any effects on other people of the ways you have 'punished' them? Can you describe how you have felt when you have been punished?

21 *Putting yourself out*
Tell of an occasion when you have really put yourself out for someone. Were your efforts appreciated? Can you now talk about something you did for someone but were too shy to admit it to them? Have you ever tried to do a good turn that turned out disastrously, either for yourself or for the person it was intended for? What went wrong? Can you recall an incident when people have thought you have been to a lot of trouble but the opposite was the case?

22 *Responsibility*
Can you talk about a time when you have been responsible for someone – perhaps younger than yourself – and you failed in your responsibilities? Have

you ever kept quiet about something that was wrong when you should have spoken up and been unpopular? Was it worth it? What are the pleasures of being 'in charge'? And the dangers? Or problems?

23 *Routine*
Describe any routine that you particularly loathed but which you were forced to go through every day or week, at some period of your life. What made it so terrible? What routines do you like? What family or annual customs, or end-of-term customs do you like? Why?

24 *Rules*
What rules do you hate? At home? At school? Can you remember being grateful that rules existed? Can you remember a time when it seemed wrong to act according to the rules? Or when it seemed unfair to enforce the rules? Have you ever enjoyed the privilege of being 'above the rules'?

25 *Selfconsciousness*
What are you selfconscious about? Mannerisms? Clothes? Appearance? Tell of a time, perhaps when you were much younger, when this really mattered. Can you recall anything you have ever done that didn't worry you at the time but which, on looking back, must have made you look silly? Have you ever clowned about to get attention? Can you remember a time when you *were* embarrassed by what you had done? What sort of things that you did when you were young do members of your family talk about now – to your embarrassment? Have you ever lost face when performing in public, or doing anything in front of a crowd of people? Or through clumsiness?

26 *Tricks*
Describe any tricks that you have played on people. Now describe any tricks that have been successfully played on you. And unsuccessful ones? What is the pleasure in watching tricks being played on someone?

27 *Truancy*
Have you ever played truant? Why? What did you do?

Did you enjoy it? Have you ever been in any serious trouble which you can now talk about? With the police or your headteacher?

28 *Trust*

Can you retell an occasion when you have broken a promise without planning to? When you have let someone down? Can you recall a time when someone has let you down? Did they realise? Or do it deliberately? Can you think of anyone you would always trust? What is it about them that makes this so?

29 *Truth*

Talk about a time when you have told the truth and not been believed. Or about a time you have lied, successfully. Why were you successful, or unsuccessful? How do you tell whether a person is being truthful? Have you ever lied for no particular reason? What problems have you ever had as a result of not telling the truth?

30 *Work*

Can you remember a time you have enjoyed working hard? Can you describe accurately a spell of really boring work? Can you describe the satisfaction of a job well done? Describe any part-time job you have had. Have you ever done any work that involves using a machine? Was it more or less enjoyable than working with your hands? Why? What sort of job would you like? Why?

How's it going?

As you gain experience and confidence in talking easily on set topics, you will need to check how effectively you are talking – and listening.

■ Undertaking one of these activities immediately after any session of talk will help to show how well you are participating in the group:
☐ List any incidents or experiences you have had but which you had forgotten until you were reminded of them by the group conversation.

☐ Discover who can most accurately retell a memory or anecdote originally told by another member of the group.

☐ Discuss what remarks or questions you think helped to keep the conversation going.

■ After several sessions, admit a silent observer to your group. Ask him or her to note down who talks most. The observer should try to be as unobtrusive as possible but might keep a scorecard using signs like these:

+	=	short contribution
*	=	good or longer contribution
**	=	very interesting contribution
?	=	good question
??	=	useful question which started someone else talking easily
!	=	off the point

Kate	+ * * ?
Rema	? + ? * ??
Rick	! + + ! + +
Shaun	+ + ** +

Alternatively, you might be able to use a cassette recorder to tape your conversation which you could later play back while filling in your own scorecards. Compare your scoring with the rest of the group's cards.

Another method is to develop your own points system. For example, everyone might start with ten points. When listening to the tape, award yourself one extra point for each relevant contribution of at least one sentence's length. You gain two points for a relevant question, five points for telling any personal anecdote which genuinely interested the group, lose three points for going off the subject, five points for 'putting down' or shutting up another member of the group – and so on.

3 What I'm doing is...

Read the following excerpts from *The Penny World* by Arthur Barton. In the first, the storyteller is being taught by a Major Compton-Hewitt how to become a door-to-door salesman of ladies' silk stockings; and in the second excerpt the narrator tries his luck for the first time.

from: The Penny World

1

Fascinated, we watched him demonstrate the elegance and desirability of those stockings. Then the complementary virtue of sheer strength. You could, it seemed, put both fists in the ankle part and stretch it a foot wide without altering the real width one iota. You could rip a sizable pin down the entire length, and the delicate fabric remained unimpaired. Were they silk or highly tensile steel? I wondered. He showed us how to do an 'approach', playing the parts in turn of the salesman and the suspicious housewife.

2

I stumbled up the drive feeling every polished pebble through my thin shoes. The hand that I raised to ring the bell trembled. When I was halfway through a gabbled rehearsal of my approach patter the door opened so that I must have seemed to be gibbering. A young woman with an amused eye and the longest cigarette holder I'd ever seen was not in the least disconcerted. She waved me into the morning room, evidently glad of the distraction, and made me demonstrate. I muttered as much as I could remember of Compton-Hewitt's sales talk. It sounded like a third-rate parody. When I put my dithering fists into the ankle part of the stocking and jerked them outwards, there was a sharp report and a big hole appeared.

I caught my prospective customer's eye and she looked quickly down at the carpet. I tried the pin trick,

and the stocking ripped obligingly from top to bottom.
It opened out into a ridiculous filmy shape. For a
moment I felt like crying.

ARTHUR BARTON

Would you be any more successful?

■ Divide your class or set equally into salespeople
and customers. Each customer has his or her base or
'home'. Customers will be polite and inquisitive (it has
been a boring day at home and you are glad to have
someone to talk to), but equally well you are very,
very reluctant to buy something that you think might
not work or which might prove useless. Consequently
you will try to keep the salesman or saleswoman
talking and explaining what he or she is demonstrating
and selling for as long as possible.

Those doing the selling will of course be eager to
sell. They earn a percentage of what they sell. They
will introduce themselves to a customer, explain and
demonstrate what they are trying to sell – and say as
much as they can to persuade that customer to buy. If
the salesperson decides he or she is having no luck at
all at one 'house', he or she can say a polite goodbye
and move on to another house as soon as there is one
with no visiting salesperson.

Each salesperson should choose one item to sell. It
might be a new type of vacuum cleaner, hi-fi
equipment, lightweight portable television – or
something more extraordinary. For example:
- a clockwork cat that consumes household dust
- an indoor rainmaking machine (ideal for potplants)
- an invisible pocket calculator
- a tiny, clip-on engine that powers supermarket
  trolleys

After a given time, stop and discover which salespeople
have made any sales. What advice can the customers
give them?

Showing and explaining

While not everyone needs the skills of a salesperson, most of us will need a related skill: that of being able to explain how to do something.

■ Choose one of the following (or a similar fairly simple task) which you know exactly how to do and for which you can easily obtain the necessary equipment:
- fitting a 13-amp plug to an electrical appliance
- bleaching, tinting or dyeing your hair
- putting a film into a camera
- grooming or caring for a pet
- serving at tennis (or other sporting or gymnastic skill)
- using a cassette tape-recorder
- preparing a simple meal which does not involve cooking
- playing snakes and ladders or some other board or card game
- loading a computer program
- applying eye make-up
- using an electric razor
- making a particular fly for fishing
- changing a typewriter ribbon
- using a pocket calculator

Using the necessary equipment, demonstrate the skill to a partner who does not understand the process. Explain each step and the reasons for it. If necessary, repeat the demonstration two or three times until your partner is able to perform *and explain* the process.

■ Change roles and learn your partner's skill.

■ Working on your own, write down an explanation of that process or skill. Get your 'teacher' to mark or correct your written account.

How good an explanation?

Some explanations may have been very successful, others less so. Can you decide how the 'teacher' could have given more help to the learner? What did the learner find difficult? Whose fault was that?

How successful do you think the following explanation is? A bank clerk is trying to explain to a new customer how to use a paying-in slip (so that the customer can put money into his bank account) and a cheque book (so that he can take money out or pay it to other people from his account).

CUSTOMER Now what do I put on this form?

BANK CLERK The date, the code number, bank and branch, the name and number of your account.

CUSTOMER Code number?

BANK CLERK Of this branch. It's on your cheque.

CUSTOMER And bank?

BANK CLERK The name of this bank.

CUSTOMER And my account number?

BANK CLERK That's on your cheques as well. And then you fill in a breakdown of coin which might comprise the credit, coupled with cheques and postal orders. Now the cheque:

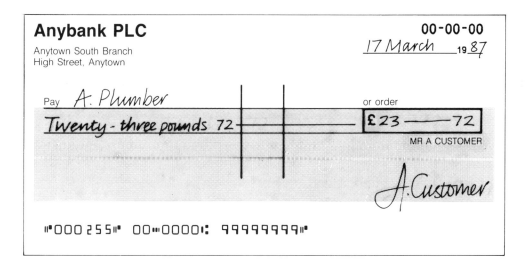

CUSTOMER This is where I find the account number –

BANK CLERK [*pointing*] That's the number of the individual cheque, then comes the code number of this branch and it's printed at the top as well, and then your account number. Now you write in the payee's name where it says 'Pay...' and of course the date, that's the date of issue; and the drawer, that's yourself, signs it in the bottom right-hand corner. Then to comply with our requirements, the amount you're paying has to agree in words and figures; that is the words in figures which you enter in the appropriate box must agree with the amount in words, written out on the second and if necessary third lines here.

CUSTOMER I have to spell it out?

BANK CLERK You do for the pounds. Modern usage is such that usually with the pence the figures are sufficient and acceptable.

☐ What problems (if any) do you think the customer might have when he comes to use the forms?

☐ How could the bank clerk have been more helpful? For example, what does he sometimes forget?

☐ What other problems might have occurred if the customer had not asked any questions?

■ Make your own blank copies of the forms. Working in pairs (with one of you being the bank clerk and the other the customer and without using this book), conduct your own explanation of how to use the forms. Once you have succeeded in this, try it again but this time the customer should say nothing except to nod or frown to show whether he or she understands or not.

At the typewriter

How successful is the following explanation or demonstration? A typist is showing students how she uses a particular typewriter to type business letters – but she is also being asked questions by an interviewer.

INTERVIEWER Now this is, er, an electronic typewriter: it doesn't have a screen and it doesn't have a memory outside it. It has got one though inside its . . . inside the actual machine.

TYPIST Yes, it has a very small memory by comparison with other mod . . . machines of its type, erm, the equivalent of about two pages of A4 typing.

INTERVIEWER A4 being the standard size of notepaper.

TYPIST Usually, yes.

INTERVIEWER So, OK, can you take us through . . . you, you're going to do one of these letters. What do you literally do?

TYPIST Yes, well because it's electronic, the first thing that needs to be done of course is for the machine to be switched on. And that may sound silly, but lots and lots of problems arise when people are trying to work the machine and it isn't switched on at the point!

This machine has the facility of an automatic paper-feed, which is this switch here, which I just pull forward and a pre-determined space . . . the paper will come up around the platen, like so, you see?

INTERVIEWER So it's now going to start typing at the sort of top left-hand corner of the paper.

TYPIST That's right. Now because it's . . .

INTERVIEWER But you don't want it there, because you've got your headed notepaper . . .

TYPIST That's right, so we must now determine where on the sheet of paper the letter itself is to be printed. If I may show you, I press the . . . the paper-key which makes the paper come around the platen, and bringing the typing-situation level with where I want to put the actual start of the letter. I'm now going to set the margin, so I press the space-bar, and I press

the key marked 'margin-set-left'. That peep indicates that the left-hand margin is set. In order to set the right-hand margin I have to press the tabulator-key, which brings the type-keys right across to the right-hand side clearing any existing setting.

INTERVIEWER So at the moment there isn't a right-hand margin in . . .

TYPIST At the moment there isn't a right-hand margin. Now I'll move across because I want it to become level with this . . . the end of this word here, lining up so it will make a nice neat right-hand margin. 'MS-Right' and that's the setting.

INTERVIEWER Now is the typewriter going to end every line in exactly the same space?

TYPIST Yes, that is the purpose of setting a right-hand margin. And I have . . . I will type this letter in what we call 'block', i.e. with a justified left-hand and right-hand margin.

INTERVIEWER *Justified* being the word that means it comes straight, in a straight line.

TYPIST That's right, instead of . . .

INTERVIEWER The letters are *justified*, they're spread out to take up the same length in each line.

TYPIST That is right, yes, that is right.

□ How has the interviewer helped that explanation?

■ Work now with the partner to whom you earlier taught a skill. You are now going to be working as a team, with your former pupil acting as an interviewer, asking questions when necessary to help your explanation. Present this to a group of other people, having first rehearsed it together. Your interviewer may keep a check list of key points which you need to make. You must talk without notes.

■ Test how successful your presentation has been by discovering if members of the watching group can now perform or explain the skill (taking account of the fact that some of them might already have been able to perform the task).

Demonstration

Almost certainly you have seen a television chef or cook demonstrating how to cook a particular recipe. You may also have seen a 'demonstrator' in a department store showing people how to use a particular gadget.

Patrick Anthony of Anglia Television

If you have ever bought a new, cheap wonder gadget after seeing a persuasive demonstration in a store, you will probably be wryly familiar with some of the strengths and weaknesses of demonstration as a teaching method. When you get the gadget home, you may well find that its use demands much more dexterity and much more practice than appeared from the effortless skill of the store demonstrator. How exactly did she persuade those carrots to fall out so quickly in such neat slices without grazing her fingers as you probably have? At what angle was the gadget held? Unless you were lucky enough to have a front-rank view you probably never saw the processes very clearly anyway.

JENNIFER ROGERS and BERNARD LOVELL

The same writers give the following advice to would-be demonstrators:

Make sure everyone can see   Some processes are so small-scale – e.g. winding hair on a roller, rubbing fat into flour, showing water-colour brush techniques, demonstrating fine cutting or grinding – that they can only be shown to individuals or groups of not more than four. Other processes – like gymnastics, yoga, or the use of large machines – can be more often successfully demonstrated to larger groups because the body movements and equipment used do not involve fine detail.

Make sure that your hands and body are not masking the crucial parts of the equipment.

Prepare in advance   Assemble everything you need before you start. Indeed it may be an essential part of the principles you are teaching that a good craftsman always has his tools set out ready, in the order he will need them.

Show the skill from the operator's point of view   If you are demonstrating the use of the sewing machine, position your students so that they are sitting behind you where they will see everything as exactly as possible from the operator's point of view. If they face you they will have to reverse mentally everything you do.

■ Keeping that advice in mind, plan and present (on your own) a *short* demonstration (with explanation) of a skill you possess to a suitable-sized group.

It would obviously be helpful if this could be done in a relevant location. For example, you may be able to use part of the Home Economics department to give a demonstration of how to prepare a particular recipe or meal; or some practical aspect of, say, child care or the making of a particular garment. Alternatively, in the art department you could demonstrate a design skill or an artistic technique. Other alternatives might suggest themselves from the CDT or a science syllabus. Or you might be able to use the PE facilities to give a

43

demonstration of a sporting skill.

Of course many skills can be demonstrated in an ordinary classroom. These might range from the demonstration of a kitchen gadget to the making of a model kit; a demonstration of how to play chess or other indoor game; a dance step or keep-fit routine; or the use of a (small) piece of equipment related to one of your hobbies or interests.

Remember to plan carefully. You will not only have to organise your equipment but think of how you will begin by explaining what you are aiming to do. Don't feel that you need to keep talking all the time but do think of what explanations are really necessary if your 'pupils' are to understand how the process should be done properly.

■ After the demonstration, ask the group if they have any questions and if there is anything they do not understand.
□ How clear or how confusing did they find your demonstration?

4 And your commentator is...

Television employs endless people to tell us things: they tell us the news, the weather, the sports scores. They tell us about paintings, buildings, animals, everyday events, international crises. We learn the rules in game shows from them and the time of day and what is coming up next after the programme. Presenters come in many styles: like dog owners at Crufts we are adept at recognising the different breeds. We can distinguish the collar and tie'd seriousness of newsreaders from the dungareed idiocy of the hosts on children's programmes and pop shows. We realise 'gurus' like David Attenborough and Jonathan Miller will offer a very different style of programme from 'men of the people' like Terry Wogan.

JANE ROOT

■ Why is it funny when a newsreader gets something wrong? What would be 'wrong' with a newsreader wearing dungarees and leaping around the studio while presenting a news bulletin? Would it be equally wrong for a children's Saturday morning show to be presented by a serious announcer sitting behind a desk and smiling only at the end of the programme?

We shall return to the question of what is the right 'style' for certain occasions later in this chapter and again in the second of these two books. For the moment, it is worth noting that just because people appear on television or radio, it does not mean they are faultless communicators . . .

. . . and now a word from George Harrison, who was said to have known John Lennon very well.

CAPITAL RADIO NEWSCASTER

They've written their own number – it's an original number and it's written by themselves.

JENNY LEE-WRIGHT

The Police, down one place to number two, they just didn't make it to number one.

TONY BLACKBURN

That one sounds as if it was made in 1965 but in fact it's older than that – it came out in 1972. . . .

MIKE SMITH

Welcome to our lunchtime soirée. . . .

NICKY HORNE

It got to the stage that you could hardly open a tabloid without seeing them [John Lennon and Yoko Ono] on the front cover. . . .

NEWSBEAT

Some of these may have been simple slips of the tongue. Others may have been the result of the disc jockey not concentrating on what he or she was saying, or of ignorance.

What makes a good DJ?

■ In groups of four, discuss what makes a good disc jockey. Talk for example about the purpose of their job. Do we need speech between records? Why do most people like some DJs and not others? Is a good DJ one who talks a lot or one who does not get in the way of the music? Is what makes a good breakfast-time DJ different from what makes a good late-night one? Are they broadcasting to different audiences?

On one radio station, the manager used to hang a sign above the microphone which said, 'If you haven't got anything to say in your *ten* seconds, SHUT UP!'

■ Suppose your group is running a radio station. Devise six 'rules' for your DJs. (Will your rules vary for day-time and night-time presenters? If so, how and why?)

Foot in mouth

Sports commentators often seem to have a special gift for not quite saying what they mean. For example, the television snooker commentator, Ted Lowe, put his foot firmly in his mouth when he said, 'Griffiths is snookered on the brown which, for those of you watching in black and white, is the ball directly behind the pink.'

■ What has gone wrong with the following comments?

Bill Frindall has done a bit of mental arithmetic with his calculator.

JOHN ARLOTT

Marie Scott from Fleetwood, the 17-year-old who has really plummeted to the top. . . .

ALAN WEEKS

It's a unique occasion really, a repeat of Melbourne 1977.

JIM LAKER

It will be the first time the two countries (England and Argentina) have met in a sporting event since the Falklands War in 1982.

NEWS REPORT

The hallmark of a great captain is the ability to win the toss at the right time.

RICHIE BENAUD

Two little jumps there – one big one and one small one. . . .

DAVID VINE

This boy swims like a greyhound.

ATHOLE STILL

This is a sheer game of chess between these two players. But Borg has an ace in the pack.

MAX ROBERTSON (on tennis)

There is only one winner in this race.

DAVID COLEMAN

Some of these 'Colemanballs' (as they are described by the magazine *Private Eye*) result from the commentator's attempt to keep talking at all costs. The result is that he – it usually is a 'he' – resorts to clichés:

Should there be a goal, the crowd always 'erupts'. Goals come in various sorts – from 'soft' and 'scrambled' to 'world-class' (*'What* a goal!'). Smaller clubs are 'minnows', and when they beat one of the big clubs in non-league fixtures they become 'giantkillers'. Awarding a penalty, the referee 'had no hesitation in pointing to the spot', and the player who takes the kick invariably 'steps up'. When you hear 'he picked his spot' it means he had time to set up his shot, not a bad case of acne.

Do not be alarmed if you hear staccato bursts like 'Moran . . . Jones . . . taken short . . . Smith . . .' They are passing the ball, not water. 'The ball breaks' spells no breakage; nor does 'breaking off the head of an Arsenal player'. You may think balls are round, but they can also be square, long, short or wide ('He lofted a square ball into the area'); there are also through balls, chipped balls, 50-50 balls, intelligent balls and dead balls.

FRITZ SPIEGL in *The Listener*, 12.12.1985

In a radio interview, one sports reporter considered why this happens:

Commentators *do* mis-use language, because they are under pressure – they are commentating live, and they have to think of something to say to link one piece of action onto another. Perhaps commentators do use clichés too much because they're not very good at English, and they're not very good at thinking up the correct word in certain situations and perhaps their vocabularies aren't wide enough under pressure. But I tend to believe that the public demands its commentaries and its sports-reporting in clichés. If we say a tackle is a crunching tackle, then every football fan knows what that is.

PAT HORTON

■ Over the next few weeks, as you watch television and listen to the radio, compile your own list of broadcasters' clangers and clichés. (Some magazines give small prizes for the 'best' ones submitted to them.)

What *should* the commentator say?

This of course depends on the sport.

Listen to most horse-racing commentaries, and you'll be surprised to see they have a lot in common. The racing commentator starts, and then all he's doing really is running through the first five or six horses, nine or ten times throughout the race, with a little bit of fill-in here to link one onto the other; and occasionally he'll look to see who's at the back if anybody interesting like the favourite isn't running well. Other than that he's . . . he's describing the actions of the first half-a-dozen horses or so.

PAT HORTON

And *Night Nurse* has a narrow lead on the inside. *Night Nurse* from *Bird's Nest, Night Nurse, Bird's Nest*, then *Lanzarote, Comedy of Errors* and *Dramatist*. Four in it now; the four that matter as they come now to the second last flight – it's still *Night Nurse* in the lead and going strongly from *Lanzarote* and *Bird's Nest. Night Nurse* over, *Bird's Nest* over second, *Lanzarote* third, *Comedy of Errors* is fourth and then comes *Dramatist* as they round the final turn – *Night Nurse* looks pretty strong and he's streaked away; he's going away from *Bird's Nest* in second place, chasing him, *Lanzarote* is third, and *Comedy of Errors* under pressure, they're coming to the last flight and *Night Nurse* is the leader – Paddy Broderick looks round, *Bird's Nest* is a danger to him, they're coming to the last flight now, *Night Nurse* and *Bird's Nest* they're absolutely . . . but *Night Nurse* has the lead and he's about three lengths clear – *Bird's Nest* is rallying and *Bird's Nest* is putting in a great finish, and Paddy Broderick's looked the wrong way, Paddy Broderick on *Night Nurse, Bird's Nest* challenging, it's *Night Nurse* from *Bird's Nest* – *Night Nurse* holds the race – *Night Nurse* a brilliant winner.

PETER O'SULLEVAN

■ Practise reading Peter O'Sullevan's commentary aloud. Can you create the sense of increasing speed and excitement as you approach the finish in the same way that he does on radio?

A slower-moving sport, such as cricket, needs a different kind of commentary, as John Arlott explains:

If the cat has come out of the tavern, or the pigeons are on the pitch behind the stumps . . . this is in fact to my mind what commentary is made of. For instance, now at this moment, one might be watching the cricket, but would also talk about the gulls screeching outside and wonder if this means there's going to be a change in the weather or something like this. You've got two things . . . three things. You've got the actual mathematics of the game, they're essential, those you must keep up to date. Then you've got the mechanics of the play which you're observing. Another thing I suppose, you've got to describe the background of the play – the buildings outside, the people around the ground, and finally you've got the history of the whole game, not just this match.

JOHN ARLOTT

A cricket commentary also has its moments of excitement – but notice in this excerpt from a commentary how John Arlott follows his own advice:

Of the England bowlers, Snow has bowled fifteen overs – four maidens – one for thirty-four; Old eleven overs, two maidens, none for forty-two. . . . Here's Snow again from the Vauxhall end, he bowls to Pollock and Pollock plays this away, to third man, and that's his century! There's the applause, two boys run on to the wicket, this won't be popular and Pollock obviously does not approve of this. Pollock's century came in a hundred and thirty-seven balls in a hundred and fifty-four minutes with a six and sixteen fours. It's his eighth Test century, his third against England, the twenty-eighth of his first-class career.

JOHN ARLOTT

Occasionally, because of technical problems, a commentator may have to provide a commentary on a match only from what he can see on a television screen and not from watching the actual event.

■ When there is a match in which you know the names of most of the players on television, try turning the sound right down and providing your own commentary!
    Alternatively, you may be able to tape-record a commentary on a school match or a game being played in the school gym. More simply, you could practise commentating on a specially arranged game of, say, table-top soccer or (much harder!) on a game of table-tennis.

Peter West (with microphone)

Different voices

Commentators on different sports not only need to give different kinds of information. They seem to need different voices or accents. Pat Horton suggests, 'Class differences come into this, for example between show-jumping commentaries and Rugby League ones. It's because of the different social backgrounds of the sport.'

Rugby League

St Helens'll tackle like mad now if they haven't been doing that already. That was a knockdown by – it's all right, play on says the ref. Now he's going for the corner, hammer and tongs, he's ten yards out. No! Murphy, Murphy's dropped it! It's a goal! A drop goal to Murphy!!!

Show jumping

He bounds along like a great bouncing ball and he's
covering the ground but he's really got to move now.
Oh! By jove! He got very close to that but he strode
right over it, a tremendous jump. Now he's wasting time
going wide around the corner, oh, yes, yes, he's done it
by about just one inch, a clear round and a fantastic bit
of riding.

■ How do you think each commentary *sounded?* And
what would they sound like in each other's 'voices'?
Would they sound *right?* Do you agree with
Pat Horton?

Sometimes, the BBC and ITV audiences are thought to
want to hear different types of commentary. Certainly
this was the case some years ago when Robin Day
(then working for ITV) and Richard Dimbleby (BBC)
both commentated on the same event.

Robin Day and Richard Dimbleby covered the 1958
State Opening of Parliament, the first royal occasion
televised after the start of commercial television. Day's
commentary was brisk, dry and efficient: Dimbleby's
style its usual blend of lavish formality. Day opened by
saying 'Well it is a dull, damp morning': Dimbleby
began 'It is a grey, rather still, misty day'. Day said:
'And down there the clump of dirty grey from the wigs
of the High Court judges', while Dimbleby intoned:
'Now the cluster of judges in scarlet and ermine and
black and gold take their places...' Dimbleby finished his
commentary in classic style by saying 'The Throne
remains – rich, shining – near yet remote – the symbol of
this rare meeting of the Queen, the Lords and the
Commons – the Three Estates of Parliament. And so
begins, with ceremony that springs from the very roots
of our democratic history, the fourth session of the three
hundredth Parliament of the Realm'. Meanwhile, Robin
Day closed with the rough debunking attitude typical of
his early ITV persona: 'The Queen will go back to
Buckingham Palace. The crown will go back to the

Tower of London. All the scarlet and ermine robes will go back to wherever they came from. And Parliament will go back to work...Everyone is wondering at Westminster what government will write the next speech from this Throne. Before Her Majesty sits on it again there may be a General Election. That is when we have our say. And what Her Majesty reads from this Throne depends on what we put in the ballot box.'

JANE ROOT

■ Note any cases of broadcasters you see or hear whom you think are adapting the way they talk to what they think their audiences want to hear (e.g. presenters of young children's programmes).

Reporting

A skill closely related to that of commentating is reporting. The commentator describes an event as it happens; the reporter summarises it later (as for example the football reporter does at half- or full-time).

Many people fail to report things accurately or fairly:

MAN   There did you see that? That red car. Came straight out of that side road, never stopped, never even slowed down. Never looked! Straight into that lorry! Women drivers, I ask you, especially the young ones!

WOMAN   Them lorry drivers, they think they own the road. Just because they're driving them big trucks, they think they can go as fast as they like. That poor old lady in that brown car, she didn't stand a chance.

From such 'reports' it is possible to gather only the very basic facts of what actually happened, but why do you think the man and woman reported as they did?

In research carried out by two New York psychiatrists, 291 people were shown a film lasting 42 seconds. In it, a man (smiling) rocked a baby's pram and pulled down a protective mosquito net. He walked off as a woman approached him.

Even on such details as the time the incident lasted, the viewers' reports of what happened in the film differed wildly. The average time the incident lasted was estimated as being one minute 45 seconds – more than twice the actual time.

Why do you think this was? What do you think some people imagined they saw?

We seem to differ in the types of things we remember. Either we are good at noting small details (clothes, hair styles, jewellery and so on) or actions (such as whether people were running or walking), but rarely both. So how good an observer and reporter are you?

The reporting game

■ Work in small groups. Each group prepares a short mime of a crime – such as a bank robbery; or a street newspaper salesperson being quietly robbed by one of his or her customers; or a similar sequence at a fish-and-chip stall but in which one customer's pocket or handbag is 'picked' by another; or a row at a disco in which a girl or boy deserts his or her partner for another and in which a character is secretly knifed; or. . . .

Each player in the mime should include one 'habit' which he or she performs at least twice – but not obviously. It might be rubbing an ear, anxiously looking at a watch, fidgeting with a pen. . . . Try not to make it obvious who is the criminal.

■ Perform your mime to the other groups. Call on three or four 'witnesses' to report exactly what happened. if necessary, ask each witness if they noticed any distinctive habits of those involved.

Which is the fairest and most accurate report?

News report

You will have seen television news reports in which a journalist is filmed talking to camera as he or she reports on a particular event – the kind of report which ends: '. . . This is Jane Smith in Birmingham for *The Nine O'Clock News.*'

Working by yourself, write, learn and present a short television news report. It is to be about one of the happenings which will be reported in tomorrow's popular papers under these headlines:
- HEADMASTER'S EARLY BATH
- MOTORWAY JAM – WITH BREAD AND BUTTER
- INCONVENIENCED!
- POLICEMAN MAKES A PRETTY PICTURE
- MP OPENS JOKE SHOP
- HEROES IN SKIRTS!
- 'I DIDN'T KNOW THEY WOULD DISSOLVE' SAYS SWIMWEAR CHIEF

You are reporting for an early-evening news bulletin and your editor has reminded you that your report must not give offence.

5 Just suppose...

If you have worked through this book in order so far, you will have practised talking about things you have done in the past and things you were doing at the time you were describing them. That is, you were talking about what you know from first-hand experience. In the last chapter you began commentating and reporting 'in role', i.e. as someone else. Improvising scenes in which you play yourself in situations in which you have not yet found yourself or scenes in which you play characters other than yourself is a very good way of finding out what it might be like to be in those circumstances. It is also a way of learning to talk in different ways suitable for different occasions – and therefore of developing your oral-communication skills.

Improvisation

Improvisation is easy. There is only one rule: the second 'line' of any improvised conversation must be 'Yes'.

If you think about it, the reason is obvious. Suppose you are improvising in pairs. *A* is given the opening line:

A   Do you speak Latvian?

B   No.

A   Oh.

There is not much more to say.

A   Do you speak Latvian?

B   Yes.

A   You do?

B   Oh yes, I speak it very well.

A   How did you come to learn it?

B Oh well, er, well you see – I met this chap. A Latvian. . . .

From that point the scene can develop. By not 'accepting' the opening line, you will always bring the scene to a grinding halt or a sterile argument.

DEBBIE You were out with that Tony Lawton last night.

NINA I never was.

DEBBIE I saw you at the bus stop.

NINA I wasn't. You can't have done.

DEBBIE I did.

NINA You didn't.

DEBBIE I did.

NINA Didn't.

DEBBIE Did.

And so on.
   Accepting, saying 'yes' to an opening line, allows for all sorts of developments:

EDWARD I say, there's £200 on your back door step. In silver.

PAUL Yes, I know.

EDWARD What do you mean, 'you know'?

PAUL My grandma put it there.

EDWARD Well, what the hell did she do that for?

PAUL It's for the dog actually.

EDWARD Why – why do you give your dog £200 in silver?

PAUL We have this courier service with the bank. And my dog has been specially trained for this sort of work. We put it there for him to collect it each morning.

   [Pause]

EDWARD It must be a pretty big dog. Does it break its neck?

PAUL   No. It's a St Bernard.

EDWARD   Well even so. £200 in silver.

PAUL   Well if I can trust my grandma, I can trust my dog can't I?

EDWARD   Well, it's your dog that carries it, not your grandma.

PAUL   No, my grandma brings it from the bank.

EDWARD   And the dog takes it back. Why bother?

PAUL   It's exercise for the dog.

EDWARD   Couldn't you exercise the dog another way?

PAUL   Yes.

■ For the following exercise, work in pairs. Ideally you should be facing your partner and sitting where you are not distracted by the other pairs in your set or class. Letter yourselves A and B. A should select an opening line from the list that follows, say it to B who (whatever it is) must say at once, 'Yes, that's true' or 'Yes, I have' or whatever is suitable – and then together A and B carry on an improvised conversation. Some improvisations may last up to two or three minutes; others will quite naturally end much sooner.

■ When you have finished one improvisation, go on to a second with B saying the starting line. Subsequently move on to working with different partners.

Starting lines
- 'Is that your elephant in the car park?'
- 'I hear you've just won £5000 on the pools and given it all away.'
- 'I hear you're in the finals of *Mastermind*.'
- 'Is it true you're entering a beauty competition?'
- 'Can my friend come to your party? I'm afraid he smells a bit.'
- 'So you've just come back from the jungle?'
- 'It is *your* house that's on fire?'
- 'Did your dog really learn to play the piano?'

You may have found that some of your improvisations turned into quite funny sketches. You may be able to tape and transcribe one or write one up from memory. Discuss how it could have been improved.

■ In pairs, rehearse and present the following sketch.

sketch: The Parrot

[MAN *walks into the shop carrying a dead parrot in a cage. He walks to counter where* SHOPKEEPER *tries to hide below cash register.*]

MAN   I wish to register a complaint . . . Hallo? Miss.

SHOPKEEPER   What do you mean, Miss?

MAN   Oh, I'm sorry. I have a cold. I wish to make a complaint.

SHOPKEEPER   We're closing for lunch.

MAN   Never mind that, my lad, I wish to complain about this parrot what I purchased not half an hour ago from this very boutique.

SHOPKEEPER   Oh yes, the Norwegian blue. What's wrong with it?

MAN   I'll tell you what's wrong with it, my lad. It's dead, that's what's wrong with it.

SHOPKEEPER   No, no, it's resting, look!

MAN   Look my lad, I know a dead parrot when I see one and I'm looking at one right now.

SHOPKEEPER   He's not dead. He's resting.

MAN   Resting!

SHOPKEEPER   Yeah, resting. Exceptional bird the Norwegian blue, beautiful plumage.

MAN   The plumage doesn't enter into it, it's stone dead.

SHOPKEEPER   It's resting.

MAN   All right then, if it's resting I'll wake it up. [*Shouts into cage.*] Wake up Polly, wake up. I've got a nice cuttlefish for you, if you wake up Polly.

SHOPKEEPER   [*Jogging cage*] There, he moved.

MAN   No he didn't. That was you pushing the cage.

SHOPKEEPER   I didn't.

MAN   Yes you did. [*Takes parrot out of cage.*] Polly, Polly. [*Bangs it against counter.*] Wake up Polly, wake up . . . [*Throws it in the air and lets it fall to the floor.*] Now that's what I call a dead parrot look.

SHOPKEEPER   Well, it's stunned.

MAN   What?

SHOPKEEPER   You stunned it just as it was waking up. Norwegian blues stun easily.

MAN   Look, I've had enough of this. The parrot is definitely deceased. When I bought it half an hour ago you assured me that its total lack of movement was due to its being tired and shagged out after a long squawk.

SHOPKEEPER   Well it may be pining for the fiords.

MAN   Pining for the fiords, what kind of talk is that? Look, why did it fall flat on its back the moment I got it home?

SHOPKEEPER   The Norwegian blue prefers kipping on its back. Beautiful plumage.

MAN   Look, I took the liberty of examining that parrot and I discovered the only reason it had been sitting on its perch in the first place was that it had been nailed there.

SHOPKEEPER   'Course it was nailed there. Otherwise it would have been through those bars like a flash of lightning.

MAN   Look. Those bars are only half an inch apart.

SHOPKEEPER   The Norwegian blue is not only as strong as an ox, it's also extremely adept at fasting. If I hadn't nailed it down it would have muscled up to those bars and voom.

MAN   Look, my lad. This parrot couldn't voom if I put 4000 volts through it. It's bleeding demised.

SHOPKEEPER   It's pining.

MAN   It's not pining, it's passed on. This parrot is no more. It's ceased to be. It's expired. It's gone to meet its maker. This is a late parrot. It's a stiff. Bereft of life it rests in peace. It would be pushing up the daisies if you hadn't nailed it to the perch. It's rung down the curtain and joined the choir invisible. It's an ex-parrot.

SHOPKEEPER Well, I'd better replace it then.

MAN [*To camera*] If you want to get anything done in this country you've got to complain till you're blue in the mouth . . .

SHOPKEEPER D'you want to come back to my place?

[*Pause.*]

MAN Yeah, all right! [*They exit.*]

JOHN CLEESE and GRAHAM CHAPMAN © Python Productions

Such 'joke' improvisations are in some ways the easiest. Because the situation is so unlikely, there is no danger of 'getting it wrong'.

■ Working in pairs, as before, try improvising from one or more of these starting lines:
- 'Is Aunt Jane really coming to live with us? She's so crabby!'
- 'Excuse me, St Peter, but am I really meant to be dead?'
- 'Tell me, Headteacher, is it really necessary to suspend my son?'
- 'So you're inviting me to appear on your television chat show?'

Notice that each of those starting lines has dictated that one of you plays a particular role or character.

From now on, decide the location of each improvisation before starting. It could be a place where two strangers might strike up a conversation – such as a park bench, a dentist's or doctor's waiting room, an airport departure lounge, on a bus or train, at a bus stop, in a café or fast-food shop, or somewhere relevant to the scene you are to play.

■ In pairs, select one of these locations or an equally suitable one you both know. *B* sits or stands 'on location'. *A* moves away and decides who *B* is. It should be someone well-known (e.g. from television, the world of sport, politics, or perhaps a local personality). After a while, A saunters slowly up to B and talks about the weather for a while and then says, 'Excuse me, I hope you don't mind my mentioning this but aren't you . . .?' B must of course say something like, 'Well yes, as a matter of fact, I am.'

Carry on the conversation. (B should not attempt a 'comic' imitation of that person's voice.) During the conversation, A might try to 'borrow' money or something belonging to B. A should decide in advance whether this is for commercial gain or whether it is because of a genuine and respectable hard-luck story. B should try to discover whether A is genuine or working a 'con'.

■ Repeat, with roles reversed.

In the mood

You will have noticed that people talk in different ways on different occasions. How they talk often depends on whom they are talking to. For example, a teacher is unlikely to talk to the headteacher or a school governor in the same way that he or she will talk to an unruly fourth-year class on a bad Monday morning. You talk differently (and not just about different things) when you are with a small group of your best friends compared with times when you are at, say, your grandparents'. You almost certainly talk differently in the doctor's surgery from the way you do in your local record shop.

The way we talk is also altered by our moods. A person with a bad headache and money worries is likely to sound very different from one who has just heard some very good news. You are probably very skilful at detecting peoples' moods from the ways they talk and indeed from their body language. How, for example, do you tell what mood your teachers are in?

■ Try the following improvisations, again in pairs. Before starting each one, think how the character you are playing might talk (and move). Remember: whoever speaks second must say 'yes' to the opening line.

1 *Join the team*
Scene: a back garden on a sunny summer's afternoon.

A has just fed well, is feeling very lazy and happy, and is looking forward to spending the afternoon reading a very amusing book.

B is a friend of A's. B is feeling cheerful and energetic and is trying to make up numbers for a game of cricket/soccer/tennis doubles. . . .

B has the opening line: 'Are you in a good mood?'

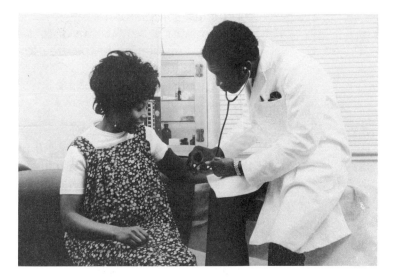

2 *At the doctor's (1)*
The doctor is busy, hard-worked and worried about fitting in all his or her calls after finishing seeing patients in the surgery, but is also concerned to spot any serious illness.

The patient is really afraid that he or she might have a very serious illness – yet also hates talking about the illness so tries talking about all sorts of other topics. . . .

The doctor has the opening line: 'So you've something you want to tell me?'

3 *At the doctor's (2)*
This time the doctor is in no hurry at all. Indeed the

doctor is as sympathetic as possible. The patient however is keen to play down the idea of being seriously ill. 'Never felt fitter.' In fact the patient *is* ill but (having no wish to see the doctor) has come only because a relative insisted.

The patient has the opening line: 'Morning, doctor. I expect you're looking forward to playing golf this afternoon?'

4 *At the dentist's*

The patient has serious toothache but is scared stiff of being hurt. What is more, the patient is convinced that he or she might easily catch a serious infection from the dentist's implements.

The dentist is new to the district and is trying to build up a reputation in the area for being especially kind and understanding. . . .

The dentist has the opening line: 'So you've had this toothache for three days now?'

5 *After the exam*

Scene: a school corridor. A and B have both taken the same examination and are also good friends.

A is quietly confident of having done well: the topics he or she revised all came up, it all seemed to go very well. B feels the opposite, despite having worked hard all year and revised thoroughly. The questions seemed difficult, it was hard going getting anything onto the paper. . . .

A knows that B is quite clever and very hard-working but inclined to think too little of himself or herself. A's aim is to cheer up B and make him or her optimistic.

A has the opening line: 'So you revised properly?'

6 *The failure*

Scene: a coffee bar, some months later.

The results of the exam have just come out. A has passed, B has not. A's aim is to keep friends with B and to keep B thinking well of himself or herself. B has just insisted on buying another two cups of coffee (trying to be cheerful about, and celebrate, A's success). B brings the coffee back to the table and has the opening line, 'Well, I was right about failing, wasn't I?'

7 *Part-time work*
Scene: in the kitchen of an ordinary home.

A teenager, working for exams, already has a paper round six mornings a week and has now got the chance of a part-time job (Thursday evenings, two hours; all day Saturdays). The teenager wants money for clothes, travel and the like, and so is keen to do both jobs. The parent (a single parent, with little cash to spare) is determined nothing should get in the way of schoolwork.

The teenager has the opening line, 'But you know jobs are scarce and you know we're short of cash?'

8 *The invalid*
In the following scene (from a novel called *The Final Test*), a boy called Cecil – he prefers his nickname, Taters – has wandered into a large, private garden which he thought was empty. Then he sees what he thinks is an old man in a wheelchair.

from: The Final Test

'Must be an old granddad,' I thought to myself. I looked round. There was nobody else in sight. There wasn't much danger. If it was just an old man in a wheelchair I could soon outrun him. Even if he was the champion wheelchair driver of all time he'd never catch me going through those trees. I wandered over and stood in front of the chair. The blanket moved and I got a real shock. Well, two shocks really. Shock number one was that the face that came into view wasn't old at all but belonged to a boy of about my own age. That shook me a bit because I immediately thought, 'is he going to be able to run as fast as me?' The second shock was that he was really pale and his eyes looked enormous because his face was so thin.

The boy in the wheelchair asks Cecil what he's called.

Well I meant to say 'Taters' but for some reason what came out was 'Cecil'. I could have kicked myself. But then an amazing thing happened. Or rather, didn't happen. He didn't laugh. Didn't even smile. He was the

first kid in the whole world who hadn't laughed at my
name. There and then I knew that this pale-faced boy
with the long hair was really something out of the
ordinary. Anybody who doesn't laugh at the name Cecil
has got to be special, haven't they? Right away all my
embarrassment disappeared and we started talking
together as if we'd known each other all our lives.

He told me his name was Skipper and that he'd
changed it from Skipton, just like I'd done. Then when I
told him that I'd thought he was a granddad he laughed
so much he nearly fell off his chair.

'I'm an invalid,' he said, waving at the bottles and the
pills. 'We used to live in India but I got this disease so
my father and mother rented this house because the
climate was supposed to be beneficial. I have a bad
chest too,' he explained. Nobody I knew would use the
word 'beneficial' because all the kids would have
laughed but it just came naturally out of Skipper. There
was no showing off.

'Don't you go to school?' I asked.

'I've never been to school. I have a private tutor.'

GARETH OWEN

Continue their conversation to see what they can
discover about each other.

Skipper has the opening line, 'You say you've got a
private tutor?'

9 *In a wheelchair*
Penny Carter (who is in her teens) is confined to a
wheelchair. A boy her own age, Dave Hobbs, lives
next door.

from: If Only I Could Walk

Suddenly Dave had said:

'Want to go for a walk in the park?'

Penny had felt a thump of excitement. Dave was
asking her out, or as good as. Penny's older sister,
Maureen, was always being taken out, but it was the first
time a boy had invited her to go anywhere.

'Can you get out of your wheelchair in your house?' Dave asked as he steered the chair round an empty coke tin lying on the pavement.

'I can move about a bit by supporting myself on my arms but I can't stand,' said Penny.

'What's wrong with you exactly?' Dave enquired in a puzzled voice.

'Spina bifida,' Penny replied.

'Spiner what?' asked Dave. 'Sorry,' he added as he jerked the chair over a stone.

'It means my muscles don't work below my waist because something's wrong with the lower part of my backbone. I was born like that,' Penny explained. . . .

'I wouldn't mind being pushed about in a chair,' Dave said. 'No, I suppose I'd get fed up after a bit,' he decided.

Penny was silent. No one had ever talked about her handicap like this before. Most people took care not to mention it but if they did they spoke in an awkward way as if it embarrassed them. But Dave spoke quite openly making it sound ordinary.

They turned into the main road. Almost at once they reached a big, modern shopping centre. . . .

Among so many people Dave found it hard to manage the wheelchair. He caught a man's heel with one of the wheels. The man swore at Dave. Dave swore back. . . .

Now as Dave weaved the chair among the shoppers Penny hoped he wasn't feeling sorry he had brought her out. Suddenly a woman grabbed her little girl and dragged her towards a shop.

'I wouldn't have run your little girl over, I was nowhere near her, missis,' said Dave loudly.

The woman didn't answer.

MYRA SCHNEIDER

Later, Dave finds a café into which he can get the wheelchair. Improvise the conversation they have as he tries to find out more about what it is like to be confined to a wheelchair.

Penny has the opening line: 'It's harder pushing the chair than you thought, isn't it?'

10 *After the bomb*
In *Brother in the Land,* much of the north of England
has been laid waste by a nuclear attack. One of the
survivors, Kim, has been about to kill a boy who was
trying to steal from her when Danny (the narrator)
arrives and the boy escapes. This is Kim's and Danny's
first meeting.

from: Brother in the Land

She smiled and I looked at her. She was thin with long,
pale hair. Fourteen or so. She had this green dress; thin
stripes of white and green really – a school dress, and
sandals. Her toes and the tops of her feet were dirty.
She seemed nice, which is a crazy thing to say after what
she'd meant to do.

Anyway, she said, 'Had a good look, have you?'

I felt my face going red and I said, 'What were they
after you for?'

She held up the bag. 'This.'

'What's in it?' I asked. She gave me this incredulous
look.

'Food of course. What else?'

Instead of answering I said, 'My name's Danny: what's
yours?'

'Kim.'

'Where d'you live?'

She gave a vague wave. 'Over there.'

'Which street?' I persisted.

'Victoria Place,' she said. 'Why?'

I shrugged. 'Just wondered. Will you be all right
now?'

She gave a short laugh. 'Sure. Will you?'

'I mean, d'you want me to walk along with you?'

She looked at me coolly. 'Haven't you got your own
problems?'

I shrugged again. 'I guess so. But I could see you
home if you like.'

'How come you're not after my grub? Or maybe you
are?'

'No!' I blurted, angrily. 'I don't need it, we've got a
shop.'

As soon as I'd said it I knew I shouldn't have. Dad would have called it drawing attention to our luck. Be thankful for it, he kept saying, but don't draw attention to it.

She must have read the look on my face because she said, 'It's okay. I don't need your stuff either, there's a place I know near Branford.'

'What's it like?' I asked.

'What?'

'Branford.' Talking to her was making me feel real for the first time in days and I didn't want her to go. I said, 'Let's walk towards your place, we can talk as we go.'

She looked at me for a moment without speaking. Then she shrugged and said, 'Okay. But one wrong move and I split, right?'

I nodded. 'Okay.'

We started walking. The sun had dipped below the broken roofs and dusk was seeping through the little streets. 'You want to know what Branford's like?' she said. 'Gone, that's what it's like. One big bomb, one big hole, no Branford.'

'No survivors?'

She shook her head. 'Shouldn't think so. Hole must be fifty feet deep. I've been close four times and I've never seen anybody alive.'

ROBERT SWINDELLS

Continue this conversation, as they talk about what has happened and what the future holds for them, with Danny saying, 'Including your family?'

How did it go?

■ After each improvisation discuss with your partner how realistic your conversation was and note down anything either of you said that surprised you or which you had never thought of before.

■ Discuss with other pairs what they invented or 'found out' about the characters or situation. How did the various improvisations differ? Which were the most 'likely'?

Sometimes it will help to act out a scene a second time, bearing in mind points you had forgotten or not thought of before.

The type of improvisation/prediction exercise based on excerpts from novels (as in 8–10 above) can be used when you are studying other books in your English course, as a way of exploring characters and situations in those books.

Group work

Improvisations with more than two characters can be more difficult to get right.

■ As a next step, improvise in groups of three, trying some of the following suggestions.

1 *The eternal triangle*
Within your trio, A likes B, B likes C and C likes A. But A hates C, B hates A and C hates B. What happens in the following situations?
☐ You have been shipwrecked on a desert island. It was A's fault. A has the opening line (to C): 'Well, it was my fault, wasn't it?' C replies, 'Yes. . .'
☐ You are all dead, locked in a room in Hell with no escape. B and C died in a car; B was driving – and drunk. The car crashed into a bus shelter, killing both B and C – and also A (known to B and C) who was waiting for a bus. C has the opening line (to B): 'I said you shouldn't drive, didn't I?' (Remember: 'accept' the opening line.)
☐ C has two tickets for a concert this evening. It is being given by a band or group all three of you like. Last week, believing there was no chance of getting any tickets, C privately agreed with B that B and C would go if C happened to get any tickets. So who goes to the concert?

2 *Fortunes*
The three of you have inherited a fortune of £24 000

on condition that it is spent within 24 hours in ways of which you all approve. How will you spend it?

3 Reunion

Each of you decides what you think you will be doing in thirty years' time. Job? Family? Living where? Previous jobs?

By chance, you meet on a train. Talk about your school days and what each of you has done since leaving school.

A variation is to play this scene twice: first, with the future as you think it might turn out if you are unlucky and secondly as you would like it to turn out.

Discuss whether you can control what your future will be like.

4 Families

Your trio consists of three members of the same family. Decide who each of you is: e.g. teenage child(ren), parent(s), grandparent. . . . Decide also on the sort of house in which you live, names, ages, interests, etc. Improvise a scene beginning with the line, 'I don't think it's right that. . .' on a theme suggested by 'Topics for talk', numbers 2, 7, 13, 17, 18, 19, 20, 21, 23 or 24, on pages 25–30.

5 In the supermarket

This is the transcript of part of a long improvisation:

CUSTOMER Okay, I have just bought this and it's gone off. I bought it three hours ago.

SALESPERSON Have you got a receipt for it?

CUSTOMER No, I wasn't given a receipt. I took it off the shelf. I took it to the counter and paid for it. I wasn't given a receipt and it's gone off.

SALESPERSON If you wait a minute I'll go and get the manager.

CUSTOMER I can't wait for you to go and get the manager. I'm just sorry. But look, the date has expired. What do you expect me to do? Surely it's your job to check these things.

SALESPERSON Well yes it is, but I can't change it for you.

CUSTOMER   Well you're paid to do the job, aren't you?

SALESPERSON   Yes.

CUSTOMER   Well then.

SALESPERSON   I can't change it. I haven't got the responsibility.

CUSTOMER   Well give me my money back and I'll go to another shop.

SALESPERSON   I can't give you your money back because you haven't brought a receipt. I'm under no obligation to do that.

CUSTOMER   Look, I'm sorry. You saw me buy it. You sold it to me. You can exchange it.

SALESPERSON   Well if you'd like to wait a minute I'll go and get the manager. He'll sort it out for you fully.

CUSTOMER   I can't wait for you to get the manager. I haven't got this sort of time. I've got all my shopping to do.

■ Decide what item of food 'it' is. Suppose the manager turns up. The manager is quite prepared to spend all day seeing the supermarket's customers are happy. However, yesterday he or she did tell off the salesperson for not keeping to the stores' rules. Carry on the scene. . . .

Larger-group work

■ In groups of five to seven, try the following improvisations.

1 Chat show

Set up a television chat show with a host and four or more famous guests. It is the kind of show where the guests remain on stage after they have been interviewed and contribute to later interviews. Each guest should be either famous for some sort of great success or notorious for a scandal that has featured in the popular newspapers.

2 *Time traveller*
A stranger to this planet (who, nevertheless, understands and speaks English but knows little of life on Earth) arrives to his surprise amongst a group of:
– nuns or monks
– Rugby players or cricketers
– commuters
or
– a formation-dance team
They try to describe what they do and why. . . .

3 *Splitting up*
The following scene is from a novel.

from: Bloxworth Blue

They drank their tea in silence. Then:

'Martin not coming?' he asked.

'No,' she said, putting ash from the cigarette into the saucer of her cup and avoiding his eyes.

She'd have to tell him, sooner or later. He was her only family. Uncle Wilfred, her father's brother; she and he were the last remaining Armitages. She would have to tell him. That, in a way, was why she'd come. To tell the family. To 'tell the bees'. She remembered someone once saying to her: 'If you can't tell the family a thing, then that thing is probably not right.' Heavens, she thought, there's scarcely a thing I've done that's 'right' in that case. And now her only family was this old man, bent with arthritis, whom she hardly knew; her uncle Wilfred, who lived alone in Lincoln since the death of his sister, her aunt Kitty. Oh, and her children, of course. They were family too. But different. They didn't belong to the past. They were the present and the future; the bleak future. The children were part of Martin and her.

'No, Martin's not coming,' she said. Best get it over. 'I think, probably, we're splitting up.' It sounded rather bald, put like that and not at all how it really was. It sounded as though it was just something that had happened one day.

'That bugger! I never liked him,' the old man said.

'Is that all? You're not surprised?'

'When you get to seventy-five nothing surprises you much. What's he done? Gone off with his secretary?'

'Not quite.'

'But there's someone else?' She didn't answer him. 'Do the kids know?'

'It's not definite. They think he's away working. Which he is. Area Manager. We didn't want to move because of Caro's O-levels. And Jason is settled now. We had a bad patch, you know.'

'Not that I really knew him, of course. He only ever came that one time.'

WILLIAM CORLETT

Caro is seventeen, Jason thirteen. Their mother's name is Judith. Work in groups of five (Judith, Uncle Wilfred, Caro, Jason and Martin), but improvise a series of conversations involving different combinations of any *three* characters about what happened and what might happen next.

4 *Nathan*

from: Nathan's True Self

At school the next day, Nathan was summoned to the Headmaster's office.

'I have had a very serious report about you,' said Mr Lombard, staring at Nathan over the top of his spectacles. 'One of our Governors, Mrs Selsdon, saw two boys last night, interfering with her car. She recognised one of them as you.'

Nathan looked shocked. 'No, sir,' he said.

'Mrs Selsdon is in no doubt,' said Mr Lombard gravely. 'She has seen you in several school plays over the years, and she is frequently in the building.'

So that was why her face looked familiar. Nathan shook his head in injured innocence as he waited for the inevitable question. It came.

'Where *were* you last night?' asked Mr Lombard.

Nathan aimed at a mixture of pride and boyish embarrassment. It was not difficult to achieve. 'I went round to see Kate Lee,' he said.

Mr Lombard gave a faint sigh. 'And she will of course testify to that,' he said.

'I expect so,' said Nathan easily as he met the Headmaster's eye. 'I mean, it *is* true.'

Mr Lombard sat back in his chair. 'If it were not for your association with Gavin Egerton, Nathan, I would be inclined to believe you,' he said. 'As it is, I do not. And I can only advise you to get out of this game you are playing while you still can. It's very dangerous.'

Nathan allowed utter bewilderment to spread across his face, but Mr Lombard was not impressed. 'You can go,' he said coldly. As Nathan turned to the door, he added, 'The boy with you was Gavin, I suppose?'

But Nathan had not relaxed his guard. 'When I go to see my girl-friend, sir, I don't take anyone with me,' he said smoothly.

'Get out of here,' said Mr Lombard.

*　　*　　*

Nathan closed the Headmaster's door behind him, more shaken by the interview than he had admitted.

ALISON PRINCE

Work in groups of five (the head, Nathan, Gavin, Kate Lee and Mrs Selsdon). Nathan and Gavin decide privately what they hoped to do to the car. Mrs Selsdon should decide, also privately, what she saw them doing. As a group, plan the order in which the characters will meet each other next and where each meeting will take place. Then improvise the meetings.

Social drama

Improvisation is also a useful way of discovering what might happen in situations in which you could, one day, really find yourself. Think of the likely characters involved in each of the following situations. Improvise each scene.

☐ Booking theatre and cinema seats; making travel arrangements.

☐ Complimenting, congratulating and praising people; and accepting the same.

☐ Dances/'discos': organising; compering; taking a partner to a fairly formal dance.

☐ Hospital visiting.

☐ Parties: planning, inviting and welcoming guests and celebrities.

☐ Restaurants: booking; arriving; ordering; table manners; paying and tipping; looking after a guest.

6 So what you're saying is...

Has anything like this ever happened to you?

FRED [*at the back door*] Mum. Mum. I'm home.

MOTHER [*distant*] In here, 'dear.

[FRED *enters*]

FRED Hello Mum.

MOTHER Nice day at school dear? D'you get on all right?

FRED Yes, ta. Mum. We had this bloke. This bloke came to give us a talk. Dead interesting it was. You see –

MOTHER Pass me them scissors, dear, will you.

FRED Here. Yes, you see, what he was saying was, about after you leave school, about training for –

MOTHER Do you want a cup of tea? There's some in the pot.

FRED Mum, I'm telling you about this man.

MOTHER Now there's a nice thing. When I offer you a cup of tea. If they taught you some manners, it'd be better.

FRED Yes, Mum, I'd love a cup of tea, please. In a minute. I want to tell you about what he said.

MOTHER Who, dear?

FRED [*patient*] This man. This chap what came to school today. To give us a talk about when we leave. Mum, you're not listening.

MOTHER Yes I am dear. You carry on. I can listen while I'm sewing, you know. I may be old but I'm not daft. [*Pause.*] Well?

FRED Well, you see, what he said was –

[*She starts up the sewing machine.*]

Ah Mum, you're not listening. . . how can I – oh! –
Never mind!

[*Door slams. Sewing machine stops.*]

MOTHER Fred? Fred? You all right?

And then again, have you ever been involved in a
conversation at all like this?

DAWN And what happened to you last night? We waited
the best part of half an hour. Missed two buses.

ANDREW More like where were you? I was there dead
on time.

DAWN On time? Let me tell you, I was there from five
to seven till we got the twenty-past bus. Not a sight of
you.

ANDREW Come off it. I was in the bus shelter dead on
seven –

DAWN What d'you mean, bus shelter? Since when's
there been a bus shelter at Navigation Road?

ANDREW What are you talking about? I was at the
'Hare and Hounds'.

DAWN We agreed we'd all meet at Navigation Road and
get the bus from there –

ANDREW But we always get the bus from –

DAWN Don't you ever listen? We said we'd meet –

ANDREW At seven o'clock and I was there. So I was
listening, proves it, don't it?

So who's at fault? And if you've ever been in a similar
situation, was the other person to blame – or you?

You might think that listening to someone is easy.
But what is it really like when you have to listen to
someone – especially if they are talking for some period
of time? What's happening in each of these situations?

Making a Point . . .

from *The Times Educational Supplement*

So what's difficult about listening?

Don't say it

This simple game requires you to listen very attentively! It is played in threes and the aim is to avoid using certain words when answering questions.

■ In turn, each player puts eight questions to one other player, with the aim of trapping that player into using any of a given set of four words. During each of these rounds, the third player (who is the one whose listening skills are being tested) deducts one point from the score of the person answering each time he or she uses one of the four 'trapwords'. Each player starts with ten points.

The game can be played either with the questioners inventing questions as the game goes on; or each player can invent (and write down) suitable questions in advance. The person answering of course knows the trapwords he or she must try to avoid. Every question *must* be answered!

Round	Who questions who	Trapwords
1	A questions B	elephant zoo big in
2	B questions C	potatoes kitchen hot very
3	C questions A	goal net great just
4	A questions C	can drink fizzy more
5	C questions B	phone dial ring say
6	B questions A	radio listen on play

The scorer may deduct points for time-wasting by either of the players.

☐ Who is the most efficient scorer?

Listening for what?

■ Have one of your group or set read the following aloud once and only once while the rest of you do not look at the book. It is a list of ingredients needed for a recipe to make a turkey pie:

- 1 packet of frozen puff-pastry
- 1 cooked (frozen) turkey
- sausagemeat *or* stuffing
- streaky bacon
- tomatoes
- 1 egg

Now write down the ingredients. How many did you remember?

■ Try the same exercise a second time, but this time concentrate on remembering only those items that you think you might have to buy on the way home if you were to make the pie this evening. Don't worry about things that are likely to be in the kitchen anyway.

☐ Is this exercise easier? Why?

■ Try the second exercise with a second, longer list (the ingredients of an onion-and-celery soup):
- onion
- celery
- tomatoes
- butter
- salt
- pepper
- mixed herbs
- tomato purée
- water
- plain flour
- single cream

■ Try this last exercise again, but now with a pen and paper at hand to note anything you want to remember.

☐ Easier? Why?

Practise this type of listening when you can. For example, listen to radio or television weather forecasts, noting the forecast for your area. For a period of two or three days, note down every instruction you are given at school that requires you to do something later in the day or week.

☐ Does this help you to pay attention? That is, to make you a better listener?

How to listen

The following hints help many people to listen more effectively.

1 Don't start by thinking you do not like the speaker or that the subject bores you. Doing so will distract you and make it harder for you to concentrate.
2 Don't try to guess in advance what the speaker is going to say.
3 If you have any control over them, make sure the conditions in which you are listening are as good as possible (no dazzling sunlight, no distracting noises, no excessive heat or cold, etc.)
4 Help the speaker to talk by looking as though you are listening. (Can *you* tell just by sight whether someone is listening to you when you are talking? What's it like when they're not? Can your teacher tell when you are not listening?)
5 Think about the person who is talking. Does he or she know about the subject? Has he or she special knowledge of the subject?
6 Has the speaker a special purpose in talking? What is it?
7 What does the speaker expect of you? Your interest? Encouragement? Your answer to a question or problem? That you should remember something? That you should change your mind?

Now think about yourself – as a listener.

1 Why are you listening – or trying to listen?
2 Would it be helpful or comforting to the speaker if you show you are 'a good listener'?
3 Will you have to make some sort of spoken response?
4 Will you have to make some sort of written response?
5 Are you listening in order to learn or understand something?
6 Will you be tested on what you hear? What sort of questions might you be asked?
7 Are you listening in order to pick out key items (as in the recipe exercises)?

8 Are you listening in order to decide which points you think are true?

9 Are you listening in order to sort out which points you think are good ones?

10 Which points will it be a nuisance if you forget?

Never be afraid to ask questions at the end – especially the all-important question which will help you to check whether you have grasped the main point: 'So what you're saying is . . . ?'

Knots

Even with such hints as those above, there are times when it is hard to grasp what is being said:

from: Knots

There is something I don't know
    that I am supposed to know.
I don't know *what* it is I don't know,
    and yet am supposed to know,
and I feel I look stupid
    If I seem both not to know it
        and not know *what* it is I don't know.
Therefore I pretend I know it.
    This is nerve-racking
    since I don't know what I must pretend to know.
Therefore I pretend to know everything.

I feel you know what I am supposed to know
but you can't tell me what it is
because you don't know that I don't know what it is.

You may know what I don't know, but not
    that I don't know it,
and I can't tell you. So you will have to tell me everything.

R. D. LAING

R. D. Laing calls that poem a 'knot'. Suppose it expresses the thoughts of a student in class. Can you unravel its meaning?

Things to do

■ Keep a record during the course of a day of any speakers (among the people you meet or whom you see on television or hear on radio) who do not get through to their listeners.

■ Listen to a phone-in on local radio. Does the presenter really listen to the callers? Have they listened carefully to the rest of the programme? Has the presenter and have any callers listened carefully to the studio guest if there is one? Which of those taking part are 'good listeners'?

The Black and White

■ Rehearse and present this short play. As you work on it, decide when the two characters are listening to and answering each other – and when they are not. When does what they say have no connection with what has just been said?

[*The* FIRST OLD WOMAN *is sitting at a milk bar table. Small.*
A SECOND OLD WOMAN *approaches. Tall. She is carrying two bowls of soup, which are covered by two plates, on each of which is a slice of bread. She puts the bowls down on the table carefully.*]

SECOND   You see that one come up and speak to me at the counter?
[*She takes the bread plates off the bowls, takes two spoons from her pocket, and places the bowls, plates and spoons.*]

FIRST   You got the bread, then?

SECOND   I didn't know how I was going to carry it. In the end I put the plates on top of the soup.

FIRST   I like a bit of bread with my soup.

[*They begin the soup. Pause.*]

SECOND   Did you see that one come up and speak to me at the counter?

FIRST   Who?

SECOND   Comes up to me, he says, hullo, he says, what's the time by your clock? Bloody liberty. I was just standing there getting your soup.

FIRST   It's tomato soup.

SECOND   What's the time by your clock? he says.

FIRST   I bet you answered him back.

SECOND   I told him all right. Go on, I said, why don't you get back into your scraghole, I said, clear off out of it before I call a copper.

[Pause.]

FIRST   I not long got here.

SECOND   Did you get the all-night bus?

FIRST   I got the all-night bus straight here.

SECOND   Where from?

FIRST   Marble Arch.

SECOND   Which one?

FIRST   The two-nine-four, that takes me all the way to Fleet Street.

SECOND   So does the two-nine-one. [Pause.] I see you talking to two strangers as I come in. You want to stop talking to strangers, old piece of boot like you, you mind who you talk to.

FIRST   I wasn't talking to any strangers.

[Pause. The FIRST OLD WOMAN follows the progress of a bus through the window.]

That's another all-night bus gone down. [Pause.] Going up the other way. Fulham way. [Pause.] That was a two-nine-seven. [Pause.] I've never been up that way. [Pause.] I've been down to Liverpool Street.

SECOND   That's up the other way.

FIRST   I don't fancy going down there, down Fulham way, and all up there.

SECOND   Uh-uh.

FIRST   I've never fancied that direction much.

[Pause.]

SECOND   How's your bread?

[*Pause.*]

FIRST Eh?

SECOND Your bread.

FIRST All right. How's yours?
[*Pause.*]

SECOND They don't charge for the bread if you have soup.

FIRST They do if you have tea.

SECOND If you have tea they do. [*Pause.*] You talk to strangers they'll take you in. Mind my word. Coppers'll take you in.

FIRST I don't talk to strangers.

SECOND They took me away in the wagon once.

FIRST They didn't keep you though.

SECOND They didn't keep me, but that was only because they took a fancy to me. They took a fancy to me when they got me in the wagon.

FIRST Do you think they'd take a fancy to me?

SECOND I wouldn't back on it.

[*The* FIRST OLD WOMAN *gazes out of the window.*]

FIRST You can see what goes on from this top table. [*Pause.*] It's better than going down to that place on the embankment, anyway.

SECOND Yes, there's not too much noise.

FIRST There's always a bit of noise.

SECOND Yes, there's always a bit of life.

[*Pause.*]

FIRST They'll be closing down soon to give it a scrub-round.

SECOND There's a wind out.

[*Pause.*]

FIRST I wouldn't mind staying.

SECOND They won't let you.

FIRST I know. [*Pause.*] Still, they only close hour and and half, don't they? [*Pause.*] It's not long. [*Pause.*] You can go along, then come back.

SECOND I'm going. I'm not coming back.

FIRST When it's light I come back. Have my tea.

SECOND I'm going. I'm going up to the Garden.

FIRST I'm not going down there. [*Pause.*] I'm going up to Waterloo Bridge.

SECOND You'll just about see the last two-nine-six come up over the river.

FIRST I'll just catch a look of it. Time I get up there.

[*Pause.*]

It don't look like an all-night bus in daylight, do it?

HAROLD PINTER

■ Improvise similar conversations in which two people don't listen to each other. They could be between two tramps, a motorist and a hitchhiker or two people in a queue. (You might be able to build up the last one into a whole-class improvisation.)

□ What is it like when one person in a conversation is not listening? Remember how Fred felt?

■ So what makes a good conversation? Read this play and then describe any occasion of which it reminds you.

The Art of Conversation

Characters: Father   Mother   Son (Tim)

SON Hello, Dad.

FATHER [*Abstractedly*] Oh, hello.

SON Busy then?

FATHER Hm? Yes, I am rather.

SON What's it all about then?

FATHER Hm? Oh! It's all these wretched forms they keep sending . . .

SON Oh that sort of busy. 'Bye then.

FATHER   Did you want to ask me something?

SON   Doesn't matter. You're busy.

FATHER   No, no. You go ahead. If you want to ask me something, go ahead.

SON   It doesn't matter. It's not all that important.

FATHER   If it wasn't important, why did you interrupt me in the first place?

SON   I didn't know you were busy till I asked you, did I?

FATHER   Well, what is it?

SON   Nothing.

FATHER   Of course it's not nothing. If you've got something to say, it must be something.

SON   You're busy.

FATHER   [*Teeth beginning to clench*] Of course I'm busy. I said I was busy. But if you've got something to say, for goodness' sake say it. I can't concentrate or get anything done with you hovering around me like that.

SON   'Bye then. [*Motor noises.*]

FATHER   Now what?

SON   I'm using forward thrust.

FATHER   What?

SON   You said stop hovering, so I'm using forward thrust.

FATHER   Oh!

SON   It's a joke. Ha, Ha!

FATHER   Well, don't make jokes about what I say.

SON   Sorry. 'Bye.

FATHER   Look, come back here and tell me what it is you want.

SON   I thought you were bu . . .

FATHER   I *am* busy. But as you've succeeded in making me forget where I've got to, I'll have to start again anyway. So before I do that and get interrupted again, will you please tell me what it is you want!

SON   It doesn't matter.

FATHER [*Without threat*] I'll box your ears in a minute. Now what is it?!

SON Oh, all right. Well it's nothing much really. We stayed on in school after the bell today . . .

FATHER Have you had detention again . . .?

SON No dad.

FATHER . . . how many times do I have to tell you? Don't fool about in class. The important thing is to get your exams.

SON But, dad . . .

FATHER Don't interrupt me. I've told you over and over again – never mind what the other boys do. It's your life and you've got to live by what you put into it . . .

SON I didn't have detention.

FATHER What?

SON I didn't get detention.

FATHER Good. Well that's all right then. What's the problem?

SON There's no problem, dad. I just wanted to tell you about something at school.

FATHER Get on with it then.

SON Well, you see, we had Mr Jones for the last period today, and we had this discussion and the bell had been gone fifteen minutes and we didn't hear it.

FATHER It *must* have been an interesting discussion!

SON Yes it was. And that's what I wanted to ask you.

FATHER [*After a pause*] Go on then.

SON Well, anyway, we weren't really supposed to have old Jones, it was Maths with Sniggers really, but he was out marking the field for Sports Day and he asked for volunteers to help him and old Jones looked after the ones who didn't volunteer.

FATHER And *you* didn't volunteer.

SON 'Never volunteer for anything!'

FATHER But I thought you were keen on sport.

SON   Doing it, yeah. But not running about after old
Sniggers with a tape measure and a whitewash brush.
[*Imitating 'Sniggers'*] Now boy! What is the
circumferential difference of two ellipses whose
diameters vary by two metres!

FATHER   Still, it doesn't do any harm to show willing,
you know.

SON   I know, you keep saying. But you also say that I
should concentrate on my exams so I thought it
would be an opportunity to do some revision . . .

FATHER   That was sensible.

SON   . . . or tonight's homework.

FATHER   I see! And did you?

SON   No. That's just the point. There were only about
six of us left – all the others had gone sucking up to
Sniggers – and old Jones started this discussion
see, and we all joined in.

FATHER   Well that's quite an achievement in itself.

SON   Yeah. Well, he said that if you look at Art – that's
Art with a capital A, you know, any art, not just
paintings and drawings and that, but music and
writing and poetry and sculpture – all that jazz – well
if it's good, then it's always good, because there is
something in great art, he said, that makes it great, for
ever and always. Not just for one time.

FATHER   Yes, that *was* interesting.

SON   Yeah.

FATHER   So, in effect, he was saying that there is an
absolute in Art to which all art aspires.

SON   Yeah, I suppose that's what he meant, or
something. Do you agree?

FATHER   Oh! Ah! Yes, well, I suppose . . . basically . . .
if you take the – er – broad view, you can say that
something good *is* good – *because* it's good. That it
contains some intrinsic goodness that is evident when
you look at it – or listen to it.

SON   Well I don't.

FATHER   Don't what?

SON I don't agree. I think people decide whether something is great art or not. I think it depends on the fashion of the time and whether people tell you it's good.

FATHER Well, you don't necessarily have to believe them.

SON Oh, that's good that is! I mean if somebody teaches you that two and two makes four – which is a fact – and also tells you that Beethoven wrote great music and you ought to like it – well if you don't like it you get a sort of guilty feeling *because* you don't like it – and then you make a great thing of saying it's rubbish, or else you *pretend* to like it.

FATHER Yes, but that's just part of the business of growing up. When you're older you can make up your own mind.

SON Oh that's the answer to everything, that is – you'll understand when you grow up! That's just my point. You're conditioned towards accepting that it is a fact that Beethoven's great and that you are a philistine if you don't agree.

FATHER I think you would be.

SON I know you do. But *would* you have thought Beethoven was good if everyone had told you he was bad?

FATHER That's begging the question. *Nobody* told me he was bad because he isn't!

SON Well that doesn't prove anything. Only that nobody had the guts to disagree with anybody.

FATHER That's a stupid argument – you could say that about anything.

SON All right then. What about Indian music?

FATHER *What* about it?

SON Well do you like it?

FATHER Not very much.

SON Why not?

FATHER Well. I don't understand it, I suppose.

SON There you are, you see.

FATHER   Yes, but I'm quite prepared to admit that if I knew more about it I would find something good in some of it, just as I'm quite sure that no matter how much I studied some pop music I would *never* find anything good in it.

SON   Yeah, well, I still think trendiness has got a lot to do with it.

FATHER   Superficially maybe. But now we're having this conversation, here's something else to think about. I mean let's change the art form. Take poetry.

SON   Yuck! Do we have to?

FATHER   No, no, be serious. What would you say makes a poem a success?

SON   When it sells a million copies, I suppose.

FATHER   No, no, no. I don't just mean financially. Artistically.

SON   When lots of people like it, I suppose.

FATHER   How many?

SON   I don't know.

FATHER   A thousand – a hundred? Ten?

SON   Yeah, well, I suppose you could say that if *one* person liked it, it was a success of a sort.

FATHER   Yes, I think you could. And I think you could go further and say that if the poet is satisfied, it's a success even if everyone else loathes it.

SON   Yeah, I think that maybe that's what some of the poets *we* have to read were after anyway!

FATHER   Hm! Good point. Well it's been nice having this discussion. We must do it more often. Mr Jones certainly started something. But I must get on with my work now.

SON   Yeah, I've got my homework to do too. But I thought I'd see what you thought. 'Bye . . .

FATHER   [*Already distant*] 'Bye, 'bye, don't forget to do some revision as well . . .

[*Some time later.*]

MOTHER   Have you finished, dear?

FATHER   [*Approaching*] Yes, at last.

MOTHER   Want a cup of coffee?

FATHER   That'd be nice. You know I had a very interesting chat with young Tim earlier this evening.

MOTHER   Oh. Was he after some more pocket money?

FATHER   No, no, no. I was quite bucked actually. It's the first time we've really talked about abstracts – you know, art and the meaning of it all.

MOTHER   Mm, I say!

FATHER   No, no, don't laugh. I mean, it may sound a bit pretentious, but I really think we got quite close.

MOTHER   You mean, he agreed with you?

FATHER   Yes, well, he did as a matter of fact. That wasn't the important thing. The discussion – that was the important thing.

MOTHER   What were you talking about?

FATHER   Well, they had a discussion at school about the intrinsic values of art and he asked me what *I* thought. And one thing led to another and I asked him what made a poem a success.

MOTHER   And did he know?

FATHER   Well, he came to an agreement. What do you think?

MOTHER   I should think it's a success if the poet can say he earns his living at it.

FATHER   No, no, that's being much too mercenary. No, no, no.

MOTHER   You mean you can't have art without starvation?

FATHER   No, no. I don't think it's got anything to do with money. Tim and I agreed that a poem was a success if the poet liked it – even if no one else did.

MOTHER   Rubbish.

FATHER   What!

MOTHER   Of course it can't be a success if only the writer likes it.

FATHER   Perhaps I should have said satisfied with it rather than liked.

MOTHER It's still nonsense. You could say it *succeeded* –
as far as the poet was concerned. But success implies
a much wider appreciation.

FATHER Oh, you're just playing with words.

MOTHER Well isn't that what poetry's all about?

FATHER I thought we were having a serious discussion.

MOTHER You mean it's not serious if I don't agree with
you.

FATHER No! It's just that to me it seems that to succeed
and to be a success are much the same thing.

MOTHER Well you certainly seem to have succeeded
with Tim this evening – but would you say that makes
you a success as a father?

FATHER [*Rising and going to door*] Really that's got
absolutely nothing to do with it.

MOTHER Don't you want your coffee?

FATHER [*Going*] No thank you. There's something I
should have mentioned to Tim.

[*A short time later.*]

FATHER Hello Tim. How's it going?

SON Hm? What?

FATHER The homework. Getting on all right?

SON Oh yeah. Yeah.

FATHER That was quite an interesting discussion we had
tonight.

SON What?

FATHER The absolute truth of art and all that.

SON Oh. Yeah.

FATHER You know. I've been thinking and if one said
succeeded rather than success . . .

SON Dad, d'you mind? Not now!

FATHER What?

SON I've got all this homework to do and I'll never get
it done if you keep interrupting me.

EDWARD KELSEY

7

Pick up the phone and...

Some telephone conversations present no problems:

GIRL So in the end we stayed in and watched 'Birdman of the Planets', it was great.

BOY [*Laughs.*] So what are you doing tonight?

GIRL Don't know yet. Geoff says he wants us,to work late one day this week but none of us wants to so we're keeping him guessing. Maybe we'll do Thursday, but I'm not doing Friday for anyone.

BOY Don't blame you. Hey, did Sue ring you? She says Barry's going to buy that old banger off that guy after all.

GIRL Do what? He must be out of his mind. That salesman who was selling it's a right crook, you can tell.

BOY I told him that, but you know what Barry's like.

GIRL Yeah, you can never tell him anything. . . .

BOY So anyway, about tonight: shall I meet you from work and we'll go for a pizza?

GIRL Yeah? – yeah, that'll be nice. OK, I'll see you at six then.

BOY I'll meet you at six.

GIRL Yeah.

BOY Bye for now then.

GIRL Bye!

BOY By-ee!

COLIN SMITH

Two friends simply using the phone for a friendly conversation and to arrange a meeting. It is not always that easy, as Keith Waterhouse remembers from the days when it was not possible to dial every number. For some, you had to ask the operator to connect you.

All I wanted was to make a desperately urgent phone call to a village in Suffolk. You couldn't dial it direct. You had to go through the operator. Only the trouble was, I couldn't reach the operator. Whenever I dialled 100, all I got was a sort of dead click. The phone book tells you what to do on such occasions. For difficulties on dialled calls, it says, dial 100. It doesn't say what you should do when you have difficulty in dialling 100. I had to use my own initiative. I browsed among the available numbers – 192 (Directory Enquiries), 190 (Ships' Telegrams), and 246 8047 (Main Events of the Day in Spanish). I settled for 151 (Telephone Out of Order or Broken).

[Dialling, then ringing tone]

ENGINEER Engineers. If you're reporting a fault, there'll be nobody here until eight in the morning.

WATERHOUSE Yes, but –

[Click]

WATERHOUSE What –! I'll teach you some manners.
[He re-dials, then ringing tone]

TELEPHONIST Engineers here. Can I help you?

WATERHOUSE Oh good evening. Listen, can you tell me how to get in touch with the operator –

TELEPHONIST Dial one hundred for the operator.

WATERHOUSE Yes, I know, but the whole point is –

[Click]

WATERHOUSE I crossed 151 off my list and transferred my affections to 191 (other Telephone Enquiries).

[Ringing tone]

ENQUIRIES Can I help you?

WATERHOUSE I sincerely hope so. I've been trying to get the operator –

ENQUIRIES Dial one hundred.

WATERHOUSE Yes, I know all about that, but if you'll just let me finish my –

ENQUIRIES If you want the operator, dial one hundred and wait.

WATERHOUSE – sentence, what I'm trying to tell you is –

ENQUIRIES What's your number?

WATERHOUSE – that I've already tried to –

ENQUIRIES What's your number?

WATERHOUSE – dial the operator, and all that happens is –

ENQUIRIES What's your number?

WATERHOUSE – that I get a sort of clicking noise.

ENQUIRIES I know that already. What's your number?

WATERHOUSE You can't possibly have known that already, because I've only just finished telling you. My number –

[Click]

WATERHOUSE A couple of blazing quarrels later, someone told me to dial 198. This is an unlisted number which is probably reserved for dealing with loonies.

[Ringing tone]

VOICE Yes?

WATERHOUSE Good evening. I was told that you could put me in touch with the op—

VOICE What do you want?

WATERHOUSE I want a telephone number. What the hell do you think I want – a toasted teacake?

. . . To cut a long case of the screaming habdabs short, 198 finally got me the operator, and the operator finally got me the number of my friend in Suffolk.

FRIEND Oh, there you are. I've been trying to ring you for the last twenty minutes, but you were engaged.

KEITH WATERHOUSE

Other things can go wrong. In the following scene, Mrs Grant (who works for a firm in Lincoln) is phoning a company in London called Numbskull and Witless. They have a small switchboard where incoming calls can be switched to different extensions. It is being looked after by Mike, a young employee who has just joined the firm.

■ After reading the scene, list the things he does wrong.

MIKE   Er – HELLO!

CALLER   [*Down the line*] Good morning . . . ?

MIKE   Hello . . . yes?

CALLER   Is that Numbskull and Witless?

MIKE   That's right, yes.

CALLER   Oh good. Could I speak to Mr Witless please?

MIKE   Mr Witless. Yes – er, I don't know whether he's in, I'll just see . . .

CALLER   Thank you.

MIKE   [*To himself*] Mr Witless, Mr Witless, what's his number, there's nothing here. O God, I'll have to tell her – Hello? Are you there, miss er –?

CALLER   Mrs Grant, I'm calling from Lincoln.

MIKE   From Lincoln! Well you see, I'm afraid there's no number here for him, and I would go over to his office and tell him but you see it's over the other side of the building and I'm on Reception so I can't leave the desk.

CALLER   Oh, I see . . . Well that's kind of you but I must get in touch with him today – or his deputy would do, who would that be?

MIKE   I'm afraid I don't know, you see they didn't tell me who was who.

CALLER   But surely you know about who's in charge?

MIKE   Well, no, I mean, I only started last week and then the girl on Reception left yesterday and Mr Numbskull put me in charge here this morning, like.

CALLER   Did he. – Oh dear, well never mind. But this *is* rather important, so maybe – you could take a message and make sure that Mr Witless gets it before five o'clock?

MIKE   Oh, right, yes of course . . . .

CALLER   Would you tell him that [*phrasing it carefully*] Mrs Grant, from Thompson and Johnson's, will be arriving tomorrow at 10.45 and hopes to –

MIKE   Oh could you wait a minute please, I'll have to write all that down. . . . [*To himself*] Now, paper?

[*He looks through various papers.*]

'Progress Report', 'Directors' minutes' – I'd better not write on them. What's in the booklet? Here – the back of this envelope. – Hello?

CALLER   [*resigned*] Hello.

MIKE   Would you mind saying that again please?

CALLER Very well: 'Mrs Grant, of Thompson and J–'

MIKE [*cries out*] I don't believe it – now the pen doesn't
work!

COLIN SMITH

Using the phone

So how *should* you use the phone? First, the
technicalities:

When you speak on the telephone
Keep the earpiece close to your ear and speak directly
into the mouthpiece. Speak clearly, unhurriedly and –
unless you are talking above a very noisy background –
not loudly. If you speak too loudly, your voice will
sound distorted to your listener. Some words, on the
telephone, lose their distinction. Words with the same
vowel-sound, 'five' and 'nine', for example, can sound
alike. Consonants should therefore be emphasised.
Speak especially carefully when using figures, names and
unfamiliar words.

You are likely to be judged by your voice alone, so
what you say and the tone in which you say it can
influence the response you get. People will tend to be
more helpful if you sound friendly and are direct.

Telephone numbers
Telephones are identified by an all-figure number (e.g.
061–834 9898); or by an exchange-name and number. A
number should always be quoted exactly as it appears in
the telephone directory or on the dial-centre label of the
telephone.

Making a call
Make sure you know the correct number of the
telephone you wish to ring. If you are unfamiliar with
the sequence to be dialled, or it is difficult to remember,
it will help you to dial correctly if you jot the number
down before making the call. It will also save you time
and trouble if you make a few brief notes of the points

you wish to discuss. When you are certain of the code and number, lift the handset, listen for the dialling tone, then dial.

After dialling, there will be a pause before you hear a tone; during this time the equipment will be connecting your call. On some calls this may take up to fifteen seconds. If you hear no tone after this period, hang up, then try again.

Dialling tone
A continuous purring sound. This means the equipment is ready for you to dial.

Ringing tone
'Burr-burr' repeated regularly. This means your called number is being rung.

Engaged tone
A single high-pitched note repeated at regular intervals. This usually means that the number you have dialled is already engaged on a call, or that every line, or the equipment, is busy.

Number-unobtainable tone
A steady note which means that the number you have called is out of service.

'Lines-engaged' announcement
On some STD calls you may hear a voice saying: 'Lines from . . . are engaged, please try later'. This indicates that there is overload on the trunk lines from the town mentioned and you should replace your handset and wait a few minutes before dialling again.

If you're cut off or get a wrong number
If you're cut off on a call you have made, or get a wrong number, or do not get a connection, dial the operator and explain what has happened. She will help you to get through (and you will not be charged unnecessarily). If you repeatedly get wrong numbers, report that your telephone is out of order to the number given under 'Enquiries' in your dialling instructions.

If you're cut-off during an incoming call, replace your handset and wait for a recall. Do not call the operator.

Answering a call

Answer as quickly as you can. A delay seems much longer to the caller than it really is, and he may think you are out. Answer with your name (e.g. Joyce Smith) or, if you think it would help, with your telephone number. The caller will then know right away that he has the right connection. (In the case of an all-figure number, only the last seven digits need to be given.) To say simply 'hello' wastes time and can be annoying. If you hear Pay-tone (rapid pips) don't hang up – hang on. The pips will stop when your caller puts money in the coin-box slot. As soon as the pips stop, say who you are. If a call – any call – is for somebody else in your household it will always save time and money if you pass on any information the caller has already given you.

When you have finished a call

Always replace the handset promptly and firmly on its rest. This stops the charging equipment and clears your line so that you can make or receive another call.

Getting it together

■ To practise your telephone skills, improvise in pairs a series of telephone conversations. If you cannot use actual telephones for this exercise, improvise sitting back to back. This will still give you practise in communicating by voice alone and without any visual signs.

1 One of you should have a copy of one day's programmes from the same week's *Radio Times* and *TV Times*, or a copy of a day's television listings from a newspaper. Your partner 'rings' you up to find out if there is anything worth watching on television tonight.

2 One of you has a copy of a reference book, information book or encyclopedia. Allow your partner a short while to to select (privately) a topic which it covers. Your partner hands it back to you, closed. He or she then rings you up for information

on that subject. Try to keep talking as you search for the information, explaining what you are doing. Then convey the information as clearly as you can, using your own words as much as possible. Check that your partner has understood.

3 Each of you should make a copy of a blank page for a term-time week from a diary. Together, fill in at least two events for this week in which you will both be involved. Then, privately, fill in another three or four, as shown in the examples. Now phone each other up to fit in a time when you can meet for an hour or so to discuss holiday plans.

Week 29	July 1987
	Monday 13
Play tennis with Pam	
	Tuesday 14
	Wednesday 15
	Thursday 16
Late night shopping?	
	Friday 17
Last day of school!	
School disco	
	Saturday 18
	Sunday 19
	Pentacost 6
Aunt Mary's !!	

Week 29	July 1987
	Monday 13
School trip	
	Tuesday 14
	Wednesday 15
Help Mum in shop	
	Thursday 16
Don't forget tv	
	Friday 17
School ends!!!	
Shop	Disco later?
	Saturday 18
Cousin Mark arrives	
	Sunday 19
	Pentacost 6

Finding out by phone

In your area Phone Book, you'll find a page near the front like the one illustrated here.

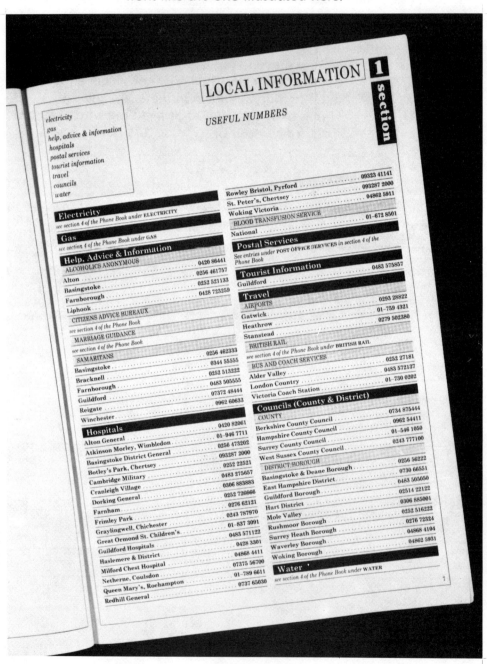

■ As practice in noting what's being said by the person at the other end of a phone conversation, get yourself a notepad and pen and then dial either your local Recipeline or Weatherline. You'll hear a tape-recorded message, giving 'Today's Recipe' or the forecast. Wait till the beginning of the message comes round and then note down the recipe or the forecast.

If you're phoning the Recipeline, note the information under two headings, *Ingredients* and *Method*. If you dial the Weatherline, note the forecast under two headings, *Forecast for the next few hours* and *Forecast for later on*.

■ To check how successful you've been in getting down the important facts, explain the recipe or forecast to a partner, using your notes. Or you could tape your own version on a cassette. Listen to it and see if it makes sense!

Try using your phone to find out other information.

■ Phone Directory Enquiries (dial 192 in most areas) to find the telephone number of a friend who lives in another part of the country. (The first thing Directory Enquiries will ask you is the name of the town in which the person lives; then his or her name, initials and address.)

■ Phone your local railway station to find the times of trains and cheapest fares for a trip to a nearby town next Saturday. (Look under 'British Rail' in your Phone Book for the number; or, in some Scottish directories, you may have to look under 'Scotrail'.)

■ Find out about local clubs and sports centres, their opening times and admission charges. For their phone numbers, look under 'Clubs and Associations – Leisure and Cultural' in your area *Yellow Pages*.

■ Use the phone to find out what's on next week at your local cinema.

Remember: have a notepad and pen handy when you make each call.

Answering the phone

With such practice, Mike should be better able to cope when Mrs Grant rings again.

MIKE   Good morning: Numbskull and Witless.

CALLER   Good morning. Could I speak to Mr Witless please?

MIKE   Mr Witless: thank you, I'll just see whether he's in his office. May I have your name please?

CALLER   Mrs Grant, from Thompson and Johnson. I'm calling from Lincoln.

MIKE   [*scribbling*] Mrs Grant from Thompson and Johnson in Lincoln. One moment please, I won't keep you waiting.

[*Click*]

WITLESS   [*on his extension*] Witless – is it urgent?

MIKE   Mrs Grant from Thompson and Johnson is on the line – *from Lincoln.*

WITLESS   Mrs Grant – ah, yes. I'm very busy now – take a message if you can.

MIKE   Yes Mr Witless.

[*Click.*]

MIKE   Hello, Mrs Grant?

CALLER   Yes, I'm here.

MIKE   I'm afraid that Mr Witless isn't available at present: could I take a message for you?

CALLER   Oh. Well, thank you.

MIKE   Ah!

[MIKE *scribbles a pencilled message as it is dictated, muttering key phrases as he writes them down.*]

CALLER   Would you say that Mrs Grant from Thompson and Johnson will be arriving at 10.45 tomorrow, and hopes to see him sometime before midday.

MIKE   . . . before lunch. Right –

[*He tears a sheet from his note pad.*]

MIKE [*reading back*] Mrs Grant from Thompson and Johnson arriving tomorrow 10.45, hopes to see Mr Witless before midday.

CALLER That's right. You will see that Mr Witless gets this before five o'clock?

MIKE It will be on his desk, Mrs Grant.

CALLER Thank you very much.

MIKE Not at all: thank you.

CALLER Goodbye.

MIKE Goodbye!

COLIN SMITH

Getting the message

Work in pairs, sitting back-to-back as before.

■ The aim is for each of you to pass a message 'by phone', as accurately as possible. For example, *A* works out what he or she wants to say in the first situation outlined below. *A* then 'rings' *B* and gives the message. *B* is in the position of Mike in the last sketch: there is nobody else available to hand the call over to. *B* must therefore take down the message as efficiently as possible. After the call, *B* writes out the message. *B* does not have to answer it. Later *A* can check its accuracy and decide whether whoever the message was handed on to could answer the enquiry.

For each call, invent a new name, address and home phone number for yourself.

Situation 1
You are phoning the vet as there is something the matter with your pet and you are wondering whether to bring it in and if so when, or whether the vet will come to see the pet. Decide on the type of pet and on what seems to be the matter.

Situation 2
You are phoning the local paper to insert a 'for sale' advertisement and want to know if the paper can

phone you back to let you know when it will appear and the cost. Decide on what you want to sell and how you will word the advertisement.

Situation 3
You are phoning the firm from which you rent a colour television. The set has gone wrong (decide on the nature of the fault or faults) and you want to know as soon as possible when someone can come round to repair it.

Situation 4
You are phoning a local hall where there are to be two concerts given by a group you very much want to see. You want to check what time each one starts, to discover what price seats are still available at each one, and at what times the box office will be open for you to buy tickets.

8 Can I begin by asking...

You may think that all you ever have to do is to *answer* questions.

- 'Why haven't you...?'
- 'When are you going to...?'
- 'What's the answer to...?'
- 'Why don't you ever...?'

In fact, it is just as important – perhaps more important – to be able to *ask* questions as to answer them. For example, in Chapter 6 we noted how important it was to ask questions such as 'So what you're saying is...' in order to check that we have understood something. It is also by asking questions that we discover information and find out why things happen the way they do. Not to be able (or not to have the courage) to get up and ask a question is to be handicapped. That way, you are limited. You don't find things out. You can't challenge what is being said when you really want to. You are deprived of your power particularly if you can't ask a question when you want to at public meetings.

Of course, you will not always get answers to your questions. A politician may not wish to admit something. Your over-worked teacher or harassed parent may be too busy thinking about something else – but part of being an effective questioner is knowing when and how to put your question.

So how do you learn to question effectively?

Question making

One way is by playing this very simple game.

■ A group selects a convenient object such as a wallchart, tape-recorder or distinctive piece of furniture. Each member of the group then invents and writes down as many questions as possible that can be asked about that object. Members of the group then come together and each person crosses out any questions which have been asked (in more or less the same words) by anyone else in the group. Also cross out any questions to which there are no possible answers at all. Score two points for each remaining question on your list and a bonus of three for the one question the group judges will produce the most interesting answer.

■ A variation of the game is to take a passage from a novel or short story, such as the one below, and invent two sets of comprehension questions about it, both sets being suitable for a class in the year below yours. One set of questions should be designed to produce the most boring answers possible; the other set (which it should still be possible to answer) should be intended to produce the most interesting answers possible.

from: The Miraculous Candidate

He looked round at the rest of the boys. Most of them were writing frantically. Others sat sucking their pens or doodling on their rough-work sheets. John looked at the big clock they had hung on the wall-bars with its second hand slowly spinning. Twenty minutes had gone already and he hadn't put pen to paper. He must do *something*.

He closed his eyes very tight and clenching his fists to the side of his head he placed himself in God's hands and began to pray. His Granny's voice came to him. 'The Patron Saint of Examinations. Pray to him if you're really stuck'. He saw the shining damp of his palms, then pressed them to his face. Now he summoned up his whole being, focused it to a point of white heat. All the good that he had ever done, that he ever would do, all his prayers, the sum total of himself, he concentrated into the name of the Saint. He clenched his eyes so hard there was a roaring in his ears. His finger-nails bit into his cheeks. His lips moved and he said, 'Saint Joseph of Cupertino, help me.'

He opened his eyes and saw that somehow he was above his desk. Not far – he was raised up about a foot and a half, his body still in a sitting position. The invigilator looked up from his paper and John tried to lower himself back down into his seat. But he had no control over his limbs. The invigilator came round his desk quickly and walked towards him over the coconut matting, his boots creaking as he came.

'What are you up to?' he hissed between his teeth.

'Nothing,' whispered John. He could feel his cheeks becoming more and more red, until his whole face throbbed with blushing

'Are you trying to copy?' The invigilator's face was on a level with the boy's. 'You can see every word the boy in front of you is writing, can't you?'

'No sir, I'm not trying to . . .' stammered John. 'I was just praying and . . .' The man looked like a Protestant. The Ministry brought in teachers from other schools. Protestant schools. He wouldn't understand about Saints.

'I don't care what you were doing. I think you are trying to copy and if you don't come down from there I'll have you disqualified.' The little man was getting as red in the face as John.

'I can't sir.'

BERNARD MacLAVERTY

What's my line?

■ The television game *What's My Line?* is also one that develops your powers of questioning. Play it in

groups of six, taking it in turns to mime a job, while one of you is questionmaster or questionmistress and the other four ask questions to discover what each job is. Questions can be answered only by 'yes' or 'no'. Each member of the team carries on putting questions until getting the answer 'no'. The questioning then passes to the next member and so on. The team is defeated if it scores ten 'no' answers before guessing the job.

Twenty questions

■ In *Twenty Questions* the team of four has twenty questions with which to guess a mystery object (which has been decided in advance by the questionmaster or questionmistress – and written down to prevent cheating). The team is given only the clue of whether the object is animal, vegetable, mineral or abstract. Answers are not restricted to 'yes' or 'no'.

Celebrity interview

■ Work in pairs. Decide on somebody famous you would both like to meet and interview. Separately, each of you then draws up a list of ten questions to put to the celebrity.

Now discuss which questions would get the most interesting answers. Produce a new list of the ten best questions.

Using these questions, improvise the interview.

■ Next, organise a 'chat show' with one host or hostess and four or five celebrities. The compere is given the relevant lists of questions to put to his or her guests. Make sure the name of the celebrity is on each list!

Your local reporter

□ Another form of interview is the one in which a newspaper reporter interviews a person who has been 'making news' in some way. Read the following two newspaper reports. Assume in each case that the reporter knew nothing about the people mentioned beforehand. What questions did he or she have to ask to get the information included in each report?

PAIR'S BLISS

Bright summer sunshine added a sparkle to Leslie and Gladys Spear's diamond wedding anniversary day.

The couple, who live at 47 Stanley Road, Wellingborough, went motor-cycling during their courting days.

Mr Spear (84) is chairman of the local over-60s club and his wife (81) is also a member.

He spent many days working in a shoe-repair business in the town followed by thirteen years driving for the Army.

The couple, who have two children, two grandchildren and three great-grandchildren retired to their present home fifteen years ago.

RICHARD'S SECOND SUCCESS

A 14-year-old Royston boy achieved a carbon-copy result in the regional final of a junior cookery contest yesterday.

Richard Bloom of Hall Lane, Royston, was runner-up in the Junior Cook of the Year competition in Cambridge – the same position he achieved last year.

Richard was competing with eight other cooks and was the only boy to reach the finals.

Although Richard is out of the national competition, his meal of smoked trout mousse, vitello Gorgonzola and Mon Ami impressed the judges with its combination of flavours and won him a Kenwood Chevette, a cookery book and other prizes.

□ Do you think the reporters could have asked more interesting questions? Such as?

■ Look for an opportunity to try your hand at being a reporter and interview someone about their work or interests. Then write up their answers into a news report which might be included in a school or class magazine.

Radio and television interviews

Normally a newspaper or magazine report does not include the reporter's questions. On radio and television we actually hear the questions as the reporter asks them.

In such interviews the interviewer is supposed to be the audience's representative. He or she asks the questions which he or she thinks the audience wants to hear answered. This is the advice one broadcaster had for would-be interviewers:

In an interview, the key thing is not so much worrying about what I'm going to ask next, but listening. I think the greatest danger is that you're so worked up about what you ask next, that you don't listen to what you're being told. You do it by trial and error. You learn that some people are not good interviewees, so you try and avoid them.

There are two kinds of radio interview, really. There are the factual ones where you want to get hold of definite points, and then you have to plan in advance. You've got to decide what are the key questions, and plan those in advance. There's the other kind of interview, where you really want to get the colour, the interest, you want to find out from that person what they are doing, and why it matters to them. Don't worry about what's going to be the next question. Then it's simply a matter of listening hard to that person and appreciating what they say, and then asking, not some cold questions you've had up your sleeve for hours, but simply what do I want to know next, what is there that I don't understand in what they were saying; what is it that I want to know more about them, what will the listener be thinking, what will the listener want to know?

And a guidebook for broadcasters adds these points:

The audience is not interested in the interviewer's ideas, so:
– don't ask long and involved questions
– don't sum up for the interviewee
– don't put your words into his mouth
– don't grunt (use body language such as a nod or smile)

BEWARE:
- of talking through the subject in too much detail immediately before recording the interview.
- of telling the interviewee in advance the questions you will ask – areas will do.
- of asking more than one question at a time.
- of asking questions that have one-word answers. Try to start the questions with either:
  Who
  What
  Where
  When
  How
  Why

Listen to the answers and respond to them in your questioning. But have your next question ready.

Now study these transcripts of two interviews, conducted by the same reporter.

■ Do you think he has followed the advice given above? Which of his questions do you think he planned in advance? Which ones obviously result from what has just been said (and therefore could not have been planned)? Is one interview more 'structured' than the other?

The first is conducted in a street outside a health-food restaurant with a group of young people.

REPORTER   You like health food?

SAM   Yeh.

CATHERINE   I don't eat, erm, any flesh, but I eat eggs, drink milk, and cheese. I don't want to eat meat because I don't think it's necessary, I don't think you have to slaughter animals when there's alternative forms.

REPORTER   What about you, Paul, are you a vegetarian?

PAUL   Yeh, I've been a vegetarian for years and years. It's mainly my sister who influenced me, and I began to think about it, and I didn't want to eat meat at all, because I think it's morally wrong.

REPORTER   To kill animals . . .

PAUL   Yeh.

REPORTER   So, but you'll eat milk . . . you eat milk and butter and things like that.

PAUL   Yeh. My sister's a vegan.

REPORTER   Can you explain what that means?

PAUL   That means you don't eat anything that is the product of an animal at all, like milk or butter or anything.

REPORTER   What about you?

ANDREW   I'm totally anti-vegetarian! I love meat and I think it's a necessary part of the human diet, and for hundreds of years people have eaten meat and there's no reason why they should suddenly stop eating it just because of morals or health reasons.

REPORTER   So what did you have for lunch today here?

ANDREW   I was dragged into a supernatural vegetarian wine bar and had rice and beans and some other insignificant bits of food that don't satisfy my appetite at all!

The second was recorded in 1984 in north-east England and broadcast in a radio magazine programme. It begins with the reporter in the studio introducing the interview that he recorded earlier.

REPORTER   And it's true, there is a lot of unemployment in the North-East. To find out just how serious a problem it is for young people I spoke to Patrick Eavis. He's the head teacher of a school in Hexham, not far from Wylam, where we began this programme. So does he think unemployment is a big problem for school-leavers in the North-East?

EAVIS   Yes it's a vast problem. Last year, last June, when the 16-year olds left school, 130 left my school in Hexham, and of that 130 only 29 got jobs. Now, all the rest of them were taken on to 1-year government schemes of one kind and another, but only 29 got full employment.

REPORTER   So what does this mean for a place like Newcastle? What happens in a city like . . . with so many young people with no work?

EAVIS   Well, the seriousness of the situation isn't yet, isn't yet realised, because it's only in the last three years that things have got really bad. But I think that really the consequences of it are almost unimaginable. Clearly there are going to be people, it seems, who will never get a job, and the effect that has on the motivation and the morale of young people is just terrifying.

REPORTER   Are they going to just stand around doing nothing?

EAVIS   Well I think if you go into Newcastle today, I think you will see lots of people doing just that, and all those pictures that we have of the North-East in the

'20s and '30s – men with caps leaning against walls and propping themselves up against Labour Exchanges – all those pictures are with us again already.

REPORTER   Is the North-East worse than the rest of the country?

EAVIS   Yes, it is worse than most of the rest of the country. There are various black areas – Northern Ireland is the worst of all, and then the North-West, which includes Liverpool, and the North-East are similarly bad.

REPORTER   Why should the North-East be as you say a black spot?

EAVIS   Er, it's because in the past it's relied on heavy industry, which is now in decline.

REPORTER   By 'heavy industry' you mean coal mining and . . .

EAVIS   Shipbuilding, heavy engineering. Now, it is these areas which have declined within the last 10 years. The iron and steel works, for example, in Consett just outside of Newcastle have been closed. The shipbuilding on the Tyne and the Wear, the Tyne Newcastle and the Wear Sunderland, have been almost, well, very very very severely reduced, causing tremendous unemployment.

REPORTER   Is there any new industry coming?

EAVIS   Yes, the Japanese car firm, Nissan, which makes Datsun cars is coming near Sunderland, but they don't intend to employ more than about 1,000 people, and of course that will not make a very great impact on the huge level of unemployment that there is in Sunderland – I understand that in Sunderland it's nearly 25% of the people unemployed.

REPORTER   The North-East is an area that has suffered.

EAVIS   Yes, it seems to suffer all the time.

□ Are there are other questions you think should have been asked?

☐ How can you tell that these are transcripts of spoken language and not written English?

■ Write up the first interview as a short article for a popular newspaper which could appear under the headline, 'MEAT TURNS OFF YOUNGSTERS'.

It's your mike...

■ In groups of four or five, select a topic in which you are all interested – either serious or light-hearted (such as a political topic, nuclear energy, fashion or pop music). Choose one of the group to be the reporter. Plan and improvise an interview (in the style of the first one quoted above) in which the reporter asks the group their views on the chosen topic. Time the interview.

■ Repeat the exercise but this time the interviewer must keep the interview to the chosen subject, see that everyone contributes *and* cover all the main points but in not much more than half the time the first interview lasted.

■ If possible, tape-record such an interview. Listen to it and discuss what the interviewer could have done to improve it.

■ If possible, tape-record an interview with an adult or someone outside the school in which you seek their views on a topical question (in the style of the second interview quoted above). Think carefully about what preparation is necessary. You may have the facilities to put these interviews together to make an audio magazine programme.

■ Make notes of any interviews on television or radio which strike you as particularly good or bad. How do interviewers' styles differ? Note that what is right for one occasion is wrong for another. The politician who is trying to avoid an issue needs questioning in a different way from, say, the victim of an accident.

Oral history

This is an account of a project in which the oral history of Jewish people living in the Midlands was recorded on tape.

Oral history is people's history, people talking about their lives and their memories. It's the first kind of history. Information has always been passed on verbally from one generation to the next, and parents and grandparents have always talked informally to young people about themselves and their family's experiences. With an oral history project – whatever the scale and level of sophistication – we are recording information to structure that natural process a little.

Oral history is about people, rather than places or specific incidents. Factual information is available elsewhere – from oral history, we get a strong sense of what life has been like for other people, what is important to them, and how they interpret what they've lived through.

Focussing on people means including other places that these people have had contact with. Interviewing the Asian community now, means exploring imperialistic links of the past and present, along with Asian culture, traditions, etc. Just so, interviewing Jews meant documenting life in Poland, Russia etc.

Overall, oral history is a real generation mixer! For example, my father and I got very close through me inviting him to tape his memories of growing up in the East End of London. Not only is he pleased at the opportunity to retell his favourite stories, and remember other memories, on the way, but *I* also learn a lot about him, and about myself, and where *I've* come from.

The question I get asked most frequently by would-be interviewers is 'But what questions do I ask??' There are no hard and fast rules as every interview is unique, and you have to think afresh each time. Basically what you are doing is assisting someone to think about themselves. Some people will require very little support to do this and an opening question like 'So you lived in

Saltley? What was it like?' will be sufficient to get them going! Open-ended questions are the ones to aim for, phrased in simple, familiar language. Be aware of the value-loaded questions – 'Would you agree that the position of Jews . . .?' – and those questions that can be answered by a straight 'Yes' or 'No'. Also guard against pushing a particular issue, when the person being interviewed obviously has other preoccupations.

Having said that, there *is* a skill in timing it correctly, so that the interviewee doesn't spend the whole session going into detail about brother-in-law Lou's septic foot! After a while, it becomes easier to pick up cues and tell you when it's OK to go on to another subject, without the interviewee feeling snubbed.

In addition, I have found it useful to use old photos as triggers, too. People's memories often flood back at the sight of familiar scenes, people etc.

■ As a major project for part of your course work, you may be able to use your interviewing skills to record the oral history of your community, perhaps writing up the memories you collect to form a small booklet.

9

And now discuss...

Rehearse and present the following playlet. An English teacher, Miss Wordsworth, has been persuaded by her fourth-year English set that, instead of spending a period writing, they should 'have a class discussion'.

Besides the reactions of the whole class, the playlet involves Miss Wordsworth and three members of the class: Wendy, Alan and the troublesome Denzo. We also hear some of the thoughts of Miss Wordsworth and Alan. It might therefore be cast with six readers, with those who read the *thoughts* standing or sitting close to their respective characters.

MISS WORDSWORTH   Right. Now, what I want us to – Denzo!

DENZO   Yuh?

MISS WORDSWORTH   Denzo, you can't join in a discussion if you're right at the back of the room.

DENZO   Don't worry miss. I'm all right here.

MISS WORDSWORTH   [thinks] He'll never join in sensibly if I let him stay there.

DENZO   Anyway I can't move the radiator, can I?

[Laughter].

MISS WORDSWORTH   [thinks] But if I insist, he'll be more of a nuisance.

MISS WORDSWORTH   Very well.

ALAN   [thinks] Denzo one; Miss Wordsworth nil.

WENDY   Please miss, what are we going to discuss?

DENZO   Sex 'n' violence!

[*Reaction.*]

WENDY   That's all you think about.

DENZO   That's why you come out with me, in'it?

[*More laughter*]

MISS WORDSWORTH   Please! If you don't keep quiet, we won't have a discussion.

MISS WORDSWORTH   [*thinks*] What a ridiculous thing to say. A silent discussion. [*Slight pause.*] They haven't noticed.

MISS WORDSWORTH   Now what we'll discuss is what we were reading about yesterday. In that story, the central character, the elder sister, she had a decision to make. A moral decision. And it's one that raises lots of important questions. Now what do you think? [*Pause.*] Alan?

ALAN   [*thinks*] She's forgotten I was away yesterday.

ALAN   Dunno, miss.

MISS WORDSWORTH   Wendy?

WENDY   [*uncertain*] I'm not sure really.

[*Pause.*]

MISS WORDSWORTH   [*thinks*] Fine start! They say they want a discussion and then when we have one, they've nothing to say.

[*Pause.*]

ALAN   [*thinks*] I wonder if the others know what we're meant to be talking about.

MISS WORDSWORTH   [*thinks*] This pressure not to be the first to say anything. . .

ALAN   [*thinks*] I'd say something if I knew what I was meant to say.

[*Pause.*]

WENDY   Miss. . . is it doing what you thinks, even if it's wrong, but if it's sort of. . .

[*Slight groan.*]

MISS WORDSWORTH   [*thinks*] Thank goodness someone's said something. Even if it is rubbish.

MISS WORDSWORTH   That's a good point. No, I think what Wendy's trying to say is, if in a given situation, we feel we have the right to break the law to achieve a greater good, because although what we may be doing is technically wrong, illegal, against the law, it is still better to do that if it will, for example, help to avoid suffering. Is that right, Wendy?

WENDY   [*meaning 'No'*] Yes.

MISS WORDSWORTH   [*thinks*] I only went on then to fill the silence.

MISS WORDSWORTH   Do you all agree with that?

[*CHORUS OF 'YES' AND 'NO'.*]

ALAN   [*thinks*] The trouble is, I don't know what I think until I've said it. And they'll all jeer if it turns out to be obvious.

MISS WORDSWORTH   [*thinks*] The trouble is, they're all afraid of being different, of saying something original.

WENDY   Please miss, can we have a vote?

DENZO   What's the good of that?

MISS WORDSWORTH   Quite right, Denzo. We'll have the vote at the end. If we ever get started.

DENZO   Miss, miss, what's a discussion for?

ALAN   [*thinks*] Well, you wanted it.

MISS WORDSWORTH   That's a good question. You answer it.

DENZO   Me?

ALAN   [*thinks*] Denzo, one; Miss Wordsworth, one.

MISS WORDSWORTH   Well, what is a discussion for?

DENZO   I dunno. Well, it's so we can sort out what we think about something. In'it?

ALAN   [*thinks*] Denzo, two; Miss Wordsworth, one.

MISS WORDSWORTH   Exactly. For sorting out what we think. But what I don't understand is, when you ask for a discussion, you have nothing to say.

ALAN   But I was away, I don't know what we're meant to be talking about.

ALAN   [*thinks*] I never meant to say that out loud.

MISS WORDSWORTH   Why didn't you say? How can you expect to join in if you don't know what we're discussing?

ALAN   [*thinks*] Exactly.

MISS WORDSWORTH   [*with new authority*] Listen, I'll tell you – all of you, and Denzo, that means you as well – I'll tell you how we'll arrange it. As a start, we'll go over the story we were reading yesterday, just in outline, retelling in our own words. Then I'll ask you to tell us about anything that's happened to you, any similar situations you've ever found yourself in, like the one in the story –

ALAN   [thinks] We still won't know 'what to say.

MISS WORDSWORTH   I know what you're thinking. But all of you can talk about what's actually happened to you. Retelling your own experience. That's straightforward.

WENDY   I'm not telling what I've done!

[Laughter and catcalls.]

ALAN   [thinks] And I'm not going to have them laugh at me.

MISS WORDSWORTH   If you like, you can always tell the story as though it happened to someone else. Change the details. But for a discussion to be really worthwhile, to get anywhere, you've got to be honest. And that can take quite a bit of courage.

ALAN   They'll laugh.

MISS WORDSWORTH   Not once they've joined in. So Denzo, you're not sitting at the back. Come and sit in the circle. Sitttt!

[Laughter and Barbara Woodhouse imitations.]

ALAN   [thinks] And the half-time score is, two all.

What experience of class discussions have you had? Have you ever had the experience of someone wrecking a good discussion by not taking it seriously? Or have you ever had to discuss something you did not know about – perhaps in a situation like this:

'We once had a discussion about bringing back hanging but no-one knew anything about it; whether the number of murders had gone up or down since the death penalty was ended...'

■ What good advice is there in the playlet above? Study it again and from it make a list of hints for running a good discussion.

■ Despite her advice, do you think Miss Wordsworth will manage to get a proper discussion going? Why? Or why not?

We shall return to the subject of large-group and class discussions in the second of these two books. For the moment we shall concentrate on discussions involving smaller groups.

Family discussions

Of course a lot of discussions happen quite naturally, often between just two or three friends or members of a family. Sometimes (as in 'The Art of Conversation' on page 89) two people have an enjoyable discussion about quite a serious subject in the course of an ordinary conversation. Other times a discussion starts up as a way of solving a problem:

SON I had to change one of my options today, Mum.

MUM Change your options? What options?

SON I changed German.

MUM To what?

SON To Drama.

MUM Drama? What do you want to do Drama for?

SON I want to act, don't I?

MUM Become an actor? But you wanted to be an air steward.

SON No, that's years ago.

DAD What does he want to do German for? He doesn't need German.

MUM Yes, but he wanted to become an air steward.

SON Well, what's German got to do with being an air steward?

MUM You've got to be able to speak different languages. And what's Drama going to do for you, in any case? Its just an easy way out of lessons for you.

SON Easy way out of lessons! We do *work* in Drama.

MUM You just run about and act like hooligans.

DAD I think he needs Drama. He's shy. I think he needs a bit of Drama to give him self-confidence.

MUM And you needn't stick up for him.

DAD He doesn't want to be a plane hostess or whatever you call them.

MUM You're just giving in to him.

SON Giving in to me? I want to become an actor, Mum.

MUM Well, you're not going to.

SON If I do Drama –

MUM [*interrupting*] The agony I went through to get you to do German.

SON I'm no good at it anyway.

MUM That's because you don't try.

SON I don't try because I don't like it.

MUM Well, if you tried you would. If you put your mind to it.

SON If I do Drama, when I leave school I may be able to go to drama college.

MUM If you think I'm paying for you to go to drama college you've got another think coming.

DAD You can't force him to do what he doesn't want to.

SON Whose life is it you're talking about?

■ Why do you think that discussion, far from solving the problem of what subjects he is to take, is turning into a quarrel? Is it simply the boy's fault for doing something without first telling his parents? Who is and who is not listening to what the other speakers say?

Solve the problem...

Holding a discussion (in a small group) is a good way of solving a problem, especially if the group concentrates on getting to the point and if each person tries not to block other people's ideas.

■ In small-group discussions, try solving the following three problems. (If possible tape-record your discussions and, later, listen to them and decide what was good and what was unhelpful in the discussions.)

Problem 1
A local council wants to double the size of a square outdoor swimming pool but there are trees growing at each corner. How can the surface area be doubled without chopping down any of the trees?

Problem 2
You drive out into the country. You park the car near a tree. You go for a walk. When you come back, someone has left a fierce dog tied to the tree. It is on a long chain and can get to each of the car doors. It won't let you get in your car. So how can you get into the car without the dog getting at you (and without hurting the dog)?

Problem 3
A man, his wife and their teenage son, together with their large dog, are on a journey. They arrive at a river. The only way across is by a small boat, which is looked after by another boy. The boat will hold two boys; one adult; or one boy and a dog. How do the family and their dog get across the river (without swimming)?

Problem 4
The following is a list of misdeeds for which you might be punished at school. It is your task to arrange them in order of increasing seriousness:
stealing; being late; leaving kit at home; bullying; cheating; writing up graffiti; being late; insolence to a teacher; untidiness; running in the corridors.

Small-group discussions

Taking part in a small-sized discussion group is a very good way of sorting out what you think about a particular topic. Though the number will vary according to circumstances, four to five people is often the best size for such groups.

It is important that you learn to trust the other members of the group and to talk honestly. This can take some courage and requires that you in turn must not 'block' or mock other people's contributions. Remember that an important part of discussion is listening. Don't shout other people down: respect their points of view and consider their opinions. Do they make sense? Are they true? Would they still be true if so-and-so were to be the case...? If you agree, say so. If not, explain carefully and sympathetically why you disagree.

Be aware that none of us really knows what we think about something until we have said it out loud. Many of us have half-formed ideas in our minds: a discussion group is a good place to try them out to see if they make sense or not. So don't be afraid to change your mind if, having said something, you later begin to disagree with what you said earlier.

But, without becoming aggressive, have the courage

131

to say what you really think. Don't just say what you think everyone expects you to say.

As you gain in confidence, alter the membership of the different groups. If you talk only with those with whom you agree, you will not meet new ideas.

In small-group discussions, it may be better not to have a leader or 'chair'. However, if you are going to have to report back your conclusions to the whole class or set, it may be helpful to have a 'scribe', a person who writes down your key conclusions.

At the start of a discussion, always check that you all know what you are meant to be discussing.

Next, share what you all actually know about the topic. Don't be afraid to describe any examples, events or personal experiences related to the subject. From such 'descriptive' talk, you can move on to saying what you think about the subject in more general terms; about what *should* happen as well as about what *has* happened.

Input
Re-read the earlier comment (page 127) about the discussion on the re-introduction of hanging. Why did that discussion fail?

Sometimes you may be given topical facts, figures and examples that will 'fuel' and inform your discussions. Other times such 'source material' will be immediately at hand – especially if you are discussing an aspect of a novel, play or poem you are already studying. But there will be times when you must find your own 'fuel' for your discussion. It may be possible to find relevant material in the school or local library or in newspapers and magazines. For example, just two or three short cuttings from a paper could extend and enliven a discussion on, say, fox-hunting:

I still remember the sick feeling in my stomach when I found the first dead hen, headless in a puddle of blood, legs asplay, feathers everywhere; then my horrified gaze slowly took in the full extent of the carnage – two, three, 40 mangled corpses hanging on the wire, sprawled inside the coop, upside down in the elder bush in the

middle of the run where one desperate bird had
scrabbled for safety. The fox had leaped the six-foot
high fence and turned the pen into a killing ground. At
that moment I would gladly have strangled that fox with
my bare hands. To let it take its chance with the hounds
would have seemed like letting a mass murderer out on
probation. ...

Animals have a right to life, hunt saboteurs say, a
right that transcends any claim that we may wish to
make upon them. So they oppose the fur and skin trade,
the use of animals in scientific experiments, even the
use of animals for food. 'Keep Death off the Plate' is a
popular sab T-shirt slogan. ... Blood sports they see
as one of the most unjustifiable forms of animal
exploitation. Hunting foxes, they believe, is cruel,
sadistic and ineffective as a method of control. ...

Hunting is cruel. It is cruel in the same way that any
form of killing animals for pleasure is cruel.

JOHN PERCIVAL in *The Listener*, 18.3.1982

Topics for discussion

The topics you discuss will normally be decided by
the other work you are doing in your course, or by
what is topical at any given time.

You may also wish to develop some of your more
informal recollections (see 'Topics for Talk', pages 25–
31) into more formal discussions from which you can
draw definite conclusions. But there will be other
times when you simply want to practise the skill of
holding a small-group discussion or to organise one
when you are going to be assessed on your ability
to take part effectively in such a group. For such
occasions, the following topics may provoke lively and
interesting discussions – but remember the need to
find topical input material for each discussion.

1 *Bullying*
How should bullying be dealt with in school? in
society? internationally? (NB Is sneaking wrong in
school?)

2 *Censorship*
Can censorship ever be right? Is there any difference
between censorship of political/sexual/violent matters?
What about censorship of young children's reading
and viewing? Dangers and advantages of censorship?

3 *Co-education*
Should co-education be compulsory?

4 *Competition*
Is competition harmful or necessary? (Compare with
co-operation.) What about school work? games?
business world? internationally?

5 *Conservation*
Local problems and issues.

6 *Crime and punishment*
Morality of one man punishing another; crime
problems; punishment at school; imprisonment;
capital punishment. 'What is effective – desirable?'

7 *Current affairs*
Topical issues (educational, social, political, economic).

8 *Doing good*
Is doing good better for the person doing it or
receiving it? What dangers can either incur? Do we
need people for whom we can do good turns? Is it
important to give to charities? How does dignity enter
this area?

9 *Dropping out*
Is it irresponsible/permissible/immoral?

10 *Fashion*
Is it important or just a commercial 'con'? What
benefits and problems does it bring?

11 *Fighting*
Is it ever sensible? Should we defend what we know is
right? Should boxing be forbidden? Wrestling? Does
fighting in a film encourage fighting in real life?

12 *Friendship*
Is friendship between girls the same relationship as
friendship between boys? What are the demands and
responsibilities of friendship? Rewards? What is a
friend?

13 *Future*
What will be the effects of the following possible
inventions: implanted artificial organs; drugs for
changing personality; primitive artificial life chemically
made; weather control; drugs to increase or decrease
intelligence; extension of life by fifty years; two-way
communication with other worlds; control of gravity;
abolition of disease?

14 *Growing up*
The problems and pleasures of adolescence.

15 *Independence*
How much independence and freedom is desirable/
possible? In one's teens/adult life/in the world at
large?

16 *Loneliness*
Hell is oneself. Hell is other people. Which is truer?

17 *Manners*
Are good manners necessary?

18 *Money*
Does money bring happiness or responsibility or
worry? Is hire-purchase immoral? Is equality of wealth
desirable or possible? Are financial incentives
necessary?

19 *Nuclear armament*
An inevitability? Its morality, compared with
conventional weapons.

20 *Old age*
What are the rights of the aged? What have they a
right to expect of society? of relatives? Does
experience automatically deserve respect?

21 *Parents*
What must be the happiness and sadnesses of
parenthood? What are the rights of a parent? The
moral duties? What are the responsibilities of a child
to its parents?

22 *Pocket money*
Should older pupils be given a grant? Should there be
legislation over the pocket-money issue? (upper and
lower limits?)

23 *Police*
What is the role of the police?

24 *Pop music*
A popular art form or commercial gimmickry?

25 *Rights*
What are human rights?

26 *Risks*
Should society legislate against the individual
undertaking a risky or dangerous activity?
(Rock-climbing, potholing, motor racing, dangerous
sports and 'dares'?)

27 *School work*
Is it the teacher's or the pupil's responsibility to see
the pupil achieves as much as he can, while at school?

28 *Scientific priorities*
Do we spend too much or too little money on space
exploration, medicine, synthetic foods and fibres,
computers, aircraft development, etc? Should priorities
be decided nationally or internationally? What were
the mistaken priorities of the past? Should politicians
or scientists make the decisions?

29 *Smoking*
Is smoking immoral, antisocial or a matter of individual
liberty? Should children be allowed to smoke? Actively
prevented? Is there a difference between smoking in
school and out?

30 *Truancy*
What are the causes of truancy? How should it be
treated?

31 *Trust*
'My word is my bond.' Can there be progress without
trust?

32 *Truth*
What are the causes of lying? Is lying ever justified?
If so, when?

33 *Violence*
Is violence ever justified? If so, when?

34 *Work*
Has everyone a right to work? Do some jobs deserve
higher pay than others?

35 *Zoos and circuses*
Discuss the arguments for and against zoos and circuses.

How did it go?

An Australian teacher, Richard McRoberts, suggests the following way of checking whether your discussion was successful:

At the end of the discussion, it is useful to review the success (or otherwise) of what has happened. Here is a checklist of questions for the group to ask itself:
- Did all members participate?
- Were their opinions/information given a proper hearing by all?
- Did all members talk to the whole group?
- Was the climate of the discussion 'supportive'?
- Were interest and involvement maintained throughout the discussion?
- Did the group stay on the topic by and large? (Brief digressions are normal, but getting right off on to another track reduces the effectiveness of the discussion.)
- Were the comments of all members clear and reasonable?
- Was it apparent whether the information presented came from personal, reported, media or research sources and did the group give appropriate weight to these sources?
- Was the consensus view of the issue formulated at the end of the discussion, or a summing up of what had been learnt offered by one or more speakers?
- Did the discussion progress through an examination of the topic and, when it had been dealt with comprehensively, come to a speedy and decisive conclusion?

If you can answer 'Yes' to all these questions, you have been involved in a most successful discussion.

RICHARD McROBERTS

10 Once upon a time...

□ Have you ever made someone genuinely laugh out loud by telling a story you have made up?
□ Have you ever really frightened someone with a made-up story?
□ Have you ever had to tell a story to someone much younger than yourself?

Paul's Tale

' " 'Ho! Ho!' said the King, slapping his fat thighs. 'Methinks this youth shows promise.' But at that moment the Court Magician stepped forward . . ." What is the matter, Paul? Don't you like this story?'

'Yes, I like it.'

'Then lie quiet, dear, and listen.'

'It was just a sort of stalk of a feather pushing itself up through the eiderdown.'

'Well, don't help it, dear, it's destructive. Where were we?' Aunt Isobel's short-sighted eyes searched down the page of the book: she looked comfortable and pink, rocking there in the firelight . . . ' "stepped forward . . ." You see the Court Magician knew that the witch had taken the magic music-box, and that Colin . . . Paul, you aren't listening!'

'Yes, I am. I can hear.'

'Of course you can't hear – right under the bed-clothes. What are you doing, dear?'

'I'm seeing what a hot water bottle feels like.'

'Don't you know what a hot water bottle feels like?'

'I know what it feels like to me. I don't know what it feels like to itself.'

'Well, shall I go on or not?'

'Yes, go on,' said Paul. He emerged from the bed-clothes, his hair ruffled.

Aunt Isobel looked at him curiously. He was her godson; he had a bad feverish cold; his mother had gone to London. 'Does it tire you, dear, to be read to?'

she said at last.

'No. But I like told stories better than read stories.'

Aunt Isobel got up and put some more coal on the fire. Then she looked at the clock. She sighed. 'Well, dear,' she said brightly, as she sat down once more on the rocking-chair. 'What sort of story would you like?' She unfolded her knitting.

'I'd like a real story.'

'How do you mean, dear?' Aunt Isobel began to cast on. The cord of her pince-nez, anchored to her bosom, rose and fell in gentle undulations.

Paul flung round on his back, staring at the ceiling. 'You know,' he said, 'quite real – so you know it must have happened.'

'Shall I tell you about Grace Darling?'

'No, tell me about a little man.'

'What sort of little man?'

'A little man just as high' – Paul's eyes searched the room – 'as that candlestick on the mantelshelf, but without the candle.'

'But that's a very small candlestick. It's only about six inches.'

'Well, about that big.'

Aunt Isobel began knitting a few stitches. She was disappointed about the fairy story. She had been reading with so much expression, making a deep voice for the king, and a wicked oily voice for the Court Magician, and a fine cheerful boyish voice for Colin, the swineherd. A little man – what could she say about a little man? 'Ah!' she exclaimed suddenly, and laid down her knitting, smiling at Paul. 'Little men . . . of course . . .'

'Well,' said Aunt Isobel, drawing in her breath, 'Once upon a time there was a little, tiny man, and he was no bigger than that candlestick – there on the mantelshelf.'

Paul settled down, his cheek on his crook'd arm, his eyes on Aunt Isobel's face. The firelight flickered softly on the walls and ceiling.

'He was the sweetest little man you ever saw, and he wore a little red jerkin and a dear little cap made out of a foxglove. His boots . . .'

'He didn't have any,' said Paul.

Aunt Isobel looked startled. 'Yes,' she exclaimed. 'He

had boots – little, pointed –'

'He didn't have any clothes,' contradicted Paul. 'He was bare.'

Aunt Isobel looked perturbed. 'But he would have been cold,' she pointed out.

'He had thick skin,' explained Paul. 'Like a twig.'

'Like a twig?'

'Yes. You know that sort of wrinkly, nubbly skin on a twig.'

Aunt Isobel knitted in silence for a second or two. She didn't like the little naked man nearly as much as the little clothed man: she was trying to get used to him. After a while she went on.

'He lived in a bluebell wood, among the roots of a dear old tree. He had a dear little house, tunnelled out of the soft, loamy earth, with a bright blue front door.'

'Why didn't he live in it?' asked Paul.

'He did live in it, dear,' explained Aunt Isobel patiently.

'I thought he lived in the potting-shed.'

'In the potting-shed?'

'Well, perhaps he had two houses. Some people do. I wish I'd seen the one with the blue front door.'

'Did you see the one in the potting-shed?' asked Aunt Isobel, after a moment's silence.

'Not inside. Right inside. I'm too big. I just sort of saw into it with a flashlight.'

'And what was it like?' asked Aunt Isobel, in spite of herself.

'Well, it was clean – in a potting-shed sort of way. He'd made the furniture himself. The floor was just earth but he'd trodden it down so that it was hard. It took him years.'

'Well, dear, you seem to know more about this little man than I do.'

Paul snuggled his head more comfortably against his elbow. He half-closed his eyes. 'Go on,' he said dreamily.

Aunt Isobel glanced at him hesitatingly. How beautiful he looked, she thought, lying there in the firelight with one curled hand lying lightly on the counterpane. 'Well,' she went on, 'this little man had a little pipe made out of straw.' She paused, rather pleased with this idea. 'A little hollow straw, through which he played jiggity little tunes. And to which he danced.' She hesitated. 'Among the blue-bells,' she added. Really this was quite a pretty story. She knitted hard for a few seconds, breathing heavily, before the next bit would come. 'Now,' she continued brightly, in a changed, higher and more conversational voice, 'up the tree, there lived a fairy.'

'In the tree?' asked Paul, incredulously.

'Yes,' said Aunt Isobel, 'in the tree.'

Paul raised his head. 'Do you know this for certain?'

'Well, Paul,' began Aunt Isobel. Then she added playfully, 'Well, I suppose I do.'

'Go on,' said Paul.

'Well, this fairy . . .'

Paul raised his head again. 'Couldn't you go on about the little man?'

'But dear, we've done the little man – how he lived in the roots, and played a pipe, and all that.'

'You didn't say about his hands and feet.'

'His hands and feet!'

'How sort of big his hands and feet looked, and how he could scuttle along. Like a rat,' Paul added.

'Like a rat!' exclaimed Aunt Isobel.

'And his voice. You didn't say anything about his voice.'

'What sort of a voice,' Aunt Isobel looked almost scared, 'did he have?'

'A croaky sort of voice. Like a frog. And he says "Will'ee" and "Doo'ee".'

'Willy and Dooey . . .' repeated Aunt Isobel.

'Instead of "Will you" and "Do you". You know.'

'Has he – got a Sussex accent?'

'Sort of. He isn't used to talking. He is the last one. He's been all alone, for years and years.'

'Did he –' Aunt Isobel swallowed. 'Did he tell you that?'

'Yes. He had an aunt and she died about fifteen years ago. But even when she was alive, he never spoke to her.'

'Why?' asked Aunt Isobel.

'He didn't like her,' said Paul.

There was silence. Paul stared dreamily into the fire. Aunt Isobel sat as if turned to stone, her hands idle in her lap. After a while, she cleared her throat.

'When did you first see this little man, Paul?'

'Oh, ages and ages ago. When did you?'

'I – Where did you find him?'

'Under the chicken house.'

'Did you – did you just speak to him?'

Paul made a little snort. 'No. I just popped a tin over him.'

'You caught him!'

'Yes. There was an old, rusty chicken-food tin near. I just popped it over him.' Paul laughed. 'He scrabbled away inside. Then I popped an old kitchen plate that was there on top of the tin.'

Aunt Isobel sat staring at Paul. 'What – did you do with him then?'

'I put him in a cake-tin, and made holes in the lid. I gave him a bit of bread and milk.'

'Didn't he – say anything?'

'Well, he was sort of croaking.'

'And then?'

'Well, I sort of forgot I had him.'

'You forgot!'

'I went fishing, you see. Then it was bedtime. And next day I didn't remember him. Then when I went to look for him, he was lying curled up at the bottom of the tin. He'd gone all soft. He just hung over my finger. All soft.'

Aunt Isobel's eyes protruded dully.

'What did you do then?'

'I gave him some cherry cordial in a fountain-pen filler.'

'That revived him?'

'Yes, that's when he began to talk. And he told me all about his aunt and everything. I harnessed him up, then, with a bit of string.'

'Oh, Paul,' exclaimed Aunt Isobel, 'how cruel.'

'Well, he'd have got away. It didn't hurt him. Then I tamed him.'

'How did you tame him?'

'Oh, how do you tame anything. With food mostly.
Chips of gelatine and raw sago he liked best. Cheese, he
liked. I'd take him out and let him go down rabbit holes
and things on the string. Then he would come back and
tell me what was going on. I put him down all kinds of
holes in trees and things.'

'Whatever for?'

'Just to know what was going on. I have all kinds of
uses for him.'

'Why,' stammered Aunt Isobel, half-rising from her
chair, 'you haven't still got him, have you?'

Paul sat up on his elbows. 'Yes. I've got him. I'm
going to keep him till I go to school. I'll need him at
school like anything.'

'But it isn't – you wouldn't be allowed –' Aunt Isobel
suddenly became extremely grave. 'Where is he now?'

'In the cake-tin.'

'Where is the cake-tin?'

'Over there. In the toy cupboard.'

Aunt Isobel looked fearfully across the shadowed
room. She stood up. 'I am going to put the light on,
and I shall take that cake-tin out into the garden.'

'It's raining,' Paul reminded her.

'I can't help that,' said Aunt Isobel. 'It is wrong and
wicked to keep a little thing like that, shut up in a cake-
tin. I shall take it out on to the back porch and open the
lid.'

'He can hear you,' said Paul.

'I don't care if he can hear me.' Aunt Isobel walked
towards the door. 'I'm thinking of his good, as much as
of anyone else's.' She switched on the light. 'Now, which
was the cupboard?'

'That one, near the fireplace.'

The door was ajar. Timidly Aunt Isobel pulled it open
with one finger. There stood the cake-tin amid a medley
of torn cardboard, playing cards, pieces of jig-saw
puzzle and an open paint box.

'What a mess, Paul!'

Nervously Aunt Isobel stared at the cake-tin. The
holes in the lid were narrow and wedge-shaped, made,
no doubt, by the big blade of the best cutting-out
scissors. Aunt Isobel drew in her breath sharply. 'If you

weren't ill, I'd make you do this. I'd make you carry out
the tin and watch you open the lid –' She hesitated as if
unnerved by the stillness of the rain-darkened room and
the sinister quiet within the cake-tin.

Then, bravely, she put out a hand. Paul watched her
absorbed, as she stretched forward the other one and,
very gingerly, picked up the cake-tin. His eyes were dark
and deep. He saw the lid was not quite on. He saw the
corner, in contact with that ample bosom, rise. He saw
the sharp edge catch the cord of Aunt Isobel's pince-nez
and, fearing for her rimless glasses, he sat up in bed.

Aunt Isobel felt the tension, the pressure of the
glasses on the bridge of her nose. A pull it was, a little
steady pull as if a small dark claw, as wrinkled as a twig,
had caught the hanging cord . . .

'Look out!' cried Paul.

Loudly she shrieked and dropped the box. It bounced
away and then lay still, gaping emptily on its side. In the
horrible hush, they heard the measured planking of the
lid as it trundled off beneath the bed.

Paul broke the silence with a croupy cough.

'Did you see him?' he asked, hoarse but interested.

'No,' stammered Aunt Isobel, almost with a sob. 'I
didn't. I didn't see him.'

'But you nearly did.'

Aunt Isobel sat down limply in the upholstered chair.
Her hand wavered vaguely round her brow and her
cheeks looked white and pendulous, as if deflated. 'Yes,'
she muttered, shivering slightly, 'Heaven help me – I
nearly did.'

Paul gazed at her a moment longer. 'That's what I
mean,' he said.

'What?' asked Aunt Isobel weakly, but as if she did
not really care.

Paul lay down again. Gently, sleepily, he pressed his
face into the pillow.

'About stories. Being real . . .'

MARY NORTON

Storytelling

■ So what makes a good storyteller? And what mistakes does Aunt Isobel make?

From your reading of 'Paul's Tale', make a list of hints for storytellers.

■ Have you ever been bored by someone telling a story that he or she thought was very interesting or exciting? (For example, has someone ever bored you by trying to retell you the plot of a film or television play?) Why was it boring? Was the story weak? Or was it the fault of the storyteller? Or was it a good story but one that did not interest you?

How good at storytelling are you?

Remember that obviously the good storyteller matches a story to his or her 'audience'. (Note how Aunt Isobel quite misjudged the sort of story Paul wanted to hear.) A story must be *right* for its audience. What is suitable on one occasion may be simply embarrassing on another.

■ Choose one of the outline stories below. Read and re-read it until you have got the plot clearly in your mind. Add as many convincing details as you can, such as names for characters. You may change the setting of the story (if one is suggested) so that it is set in an area you know. Add local street and place names. Tell the story to yourself, silently. Think how you'll pause, how you will add to it to *make it real* for your listener, how you will help your listener to 'see' the story just as Paul nearly made Aunt Isobel 'see' the little man.

■ Now tell the story (without any notes, etc.) to someone who has been working on another story. Then listen to that person's story.

Discuss how you can both improve your stories and the ways you tell them. Which parts work well? Which don't?

■ Try telling your story again to someone who has been working on a third story. Think how you may have to adapt its 'tone' to please (or avoid offending) your new listener.

Story outline 1

A young man successfully broke into a factory in New Addington, Surrey to steal cheese. The getaway was planned; he and his brother had two prams outside. Unfortunately, the two forgot one thing. It was snowing at the time and police simply followed the pram tracks.

Story outline 2

A friend, touring with a caravan on the continent, ran short of time to catch the ferry back to England, so he drove furiously through the night, with his wife sleeping in the caravan. At length, he had to stop to relieve himself, and while he was out, his wife woke up and also felt the call of nature. So she left the fastness of the caravan and went into the bushes. And her husband returned and drove off into the night. Luckily (in some ways) the next car along was a police-car, but she still had some difficulty in explaining what had happened.

Story outline 3

A friend buys two tickets in a lottery – one for himself and one for a colleague at the office. However, he forgets to give the ticket to his colleague, and, inevitably, one of the tickets wins the first prize. It is the one he had planned to give to his colleague, and he is so honest that he hands it over. 'Thanks very much', says the colleague, pockets a cool million and is never seen again.

Story outline 4

A Surrey couple had their car stolen from their front drive. Four days later it reappeared – with two theatre tickets on the front seat and a note which read: 'Sorry. We had to take your car in an emergency. Please accept the tickets with our apologies.' A few days later they used the tickets and returned to find their home stripped, even to the curtains.

Story outline 5

A friend wasn't feeling well, but just couldn't see how he could miss the office Christmas party, so he took the train to town and over-indulged himself enormously, with the result that he was really very ill in several directions at once. So on his way back to the station he stumbled into an army surplus shop and asked for a pair of trousers – '38 waist, quick, here's a fiver' – the assistant stuffed them into a bag, and the man just managed to scramble into an empty compartment on the corridorless train back home. He removed his mucky old trousers, rolled them up, and threw them out of the window. Then he opened the bag, and found that somehow he had bought a denim jacket.

Story outline 6

A woman came home one day to find her Doberman pinscher lying in the hall, choking. She got him to her car, and drove to the vet. After a quick examination he said he'd have to operate, so the woman went home to wait for news. But even as she opened her front door she could hear the telephone ringing – it was the vet who told her not to ask questions but to leave the house at once, go to the house next door, and ring him back. It turned out that he'd found a couple of human fingers lodged in the dog's throat, so he'd put two and two together and called the police. At that moment they arrived, so the woman rushed out to let them in. They searched the house, and what did they find? An unconscious burglar hiding in a cupboard ... with a couple of fingers missing.

RODNEY DALE

Reading stories aloud

It may seem easier to read a story aloud than to tell one. In fact it is often very much harder to make a 'read' story as lively as a 'told' one. Certainly nobody enjoys a reading which is just a stream of words delivered with little expression by someone whose head is buried in a book.

The following points should help you read effectively:

1 Never try to read at sight. Read it through to yourself at least once beforehand: you must understand a story yourself before you can communicate it to someone else. You certainly need to know what sort of people the different characters are, when the mood is going to change and so on.

2 Read from a position where you can be seen by all your listeners – even if that means coming out to the front of the room! It is much harder for an audience to pay attention to someone whom they cannot properly see or, worse, cannot properly hear.

3 Don't take it word by word. Scan ahead to take in whole thoughts and concentrate on the meaning of what you are reading. Don't worry about sounding 'special' or clever.

4 Really feel your way into the sense and mood of the story but don't 'ham it up' by putting on artificially sad or happy voices (remember Aunt Isobel).

5 Do open your mouth and jaw: you have got to let the sound out!

6 Speak up enough to be heard by all your listeners – but don't shout. (It is a good idea to practise reading to small or medium-sized groups before trying to hold the attention of a large class or group.)

7 Do vary the pace and volume as the sense dictates.

8 Don't be afraid to pause at suitable moments: there is usually no prize for speed-reading! (Don't overdo the pauses though.)

9 Do hold up your book or paper. Don't read to the floor with only the top of your head visible to your listeners.

10 Enjoy yourself and believe you *can* read well. Confident readers almost always make the best readers.

Stories to read

1 Don't be afraid to read aloud the stories you have written. They are the ones you know best (but you still need to practise or rehearse your reading).
2 In groups of three, rehearse a reading of all or part of 'Paul's Tale' with one of you reading what is said by Paul, one reading what is said by Aunt Isobel and one reading the narration.
3 See how effectively you can read this short fable:

from: Fables for Our Times

One afternoon a big wolf waited in a dark forest for a little girl to come along carrying a basket of food to her grandmother. Finally a little girl did come along and she was carrying a basket of food. 'Are you carrying that basket to your grandmother?' asked the wolf. The little girl said yes, she was. So the wolf asked her where her grandmother lived and the little girl told him and he disappeared into the wood.

When the little girl opened the door of her grandmother's house she saw that there was somebody in bed with a nightcap and nightgown on. She had approached no nearer than twenty-five feet from the bed when she saw that it was not her grandmother but the wolf, for even in a nightcap a wolf does not look any more like your grandmother than the Metro-Goldwyn lion looks like Calvin Coolidge. So the little girl took an automatic out of her basket and shot the wolf dead.

And the moral of that story is that it's not so easy to fool little girls nowadays as it used to be.

JAMES THURBER

(You might learn to tell this story by heart.)

4 Find other short stories or passages that you like and which you think will interest your listeners. Think how you will introduce them to your audience. Particularly if they are excerpts from longer works, your audience will need to know who the characters are and where the story is taking place.

149

Choral speech

Sometimes a poem tells a story and such 'narrative' poems are often suitable for saying or 'telling' by groups of readers. Any poem you choose to say in this way must be one that you enjoy saying, one you feel you can read well and one that will interest your listeners. It also needs to be a poem that allows opportunities for individuals to say particular lines or sections, and for 'sub-groups' or the whole group to say other parts.

■ Practise with one of the following three poems. The first requires at least four readers; the others could involve larger groups. Begin by reading the poem through silently and then discuss which lines could be given to individual readers and which might be said by groups. Practise your reading several times so that everyone becomes clear when to 'come in', and aware of how each line or group of lines needs saying and of the rhythms of the poem.

When you come to say the poem, sense whether your audience is really listening and think whether you are really 'talking' (i.e. *meaning*) the poem. Remember:
    – Listen,
    – Talk,
    – Communicate.

Elephants are Different to Different People

Wilson and Pilcer and Snack stood before the zoo elephant.

Wilson said, 'What is its name? Is it from Asia or Africa? Who feeds it? Is it a he or a she? How old is it? Do they have twins? How much does it cost to feed? How much does it weigh? If it dies how much will another one cost? If it dies what will they use the bones, the fat, and the hide for? What use is it besides to look at?'

Pilcer didn't have any questions: he was murmuring to himself, 'It's a house by itself, walls and windows, the

ears come from tall cornfields, by God; the architect of
those legs was a workman, by God; he stands like a
bridge out across deep water; the face is sad and the
eyes are kind; I know elephants are good to babies.'

Snack looked up and down and at last said to himself,
'He's a tough son-of-a-gun outside and I'll bet he's got a
strong heart, I'll bet he's strong as a copper-riveted
boiler inside.'

> They didn't put up any arguments.
> They didn't throw anything in each other's faces.
> Three men saw the elephant three ways
> And let it go at that.
> They didn't spoil a sunny Sunday afternoon;
> 'Sunday comes only once a week,' they told each
> other.

CARL SANDBURG

Poem after Prévert

We are going to see the rabbit,
We are going to see the rabbit.
Which rabbit, people say?
Which rabbit, ask the children?
Which rabbit?
The only rabbit,
The only rabbit in England.
Sitting behind a barbed-wire fence
Under the floodlights, neon lights,
Sodium lights,
Nibbling grass
On the only patch of grass
In England, in England
(Except the grass by the hoardings which doesn't count).
We are going to see the rabbit
And we must be there on time.

First we shall go by escalator,
Then we shall go by underground,

And then we shall go by motorway
And then by helicopter way,
And the last ten yards we shall have to go
On foot.

And now we are going
All the way to see the rabbit,
We are nearly there,
We are longing to see it,
And so is the crowd
Which is here in thousands
With mounted policemen
And big loudspeakers
And bands and banners,
And everyone has come a long way.
But soon we shall see it
Sitting and nibbling
The blades of grass
In – but something has gone wrong!
Why is everyone so angry,
Why is everyone jostling
And slanging and complaining?

The rabbit has gone,
Yes, the rabbit has gone.
He has actually burrowed down into the earth
And made himself a warren, under the earth,
Despite all these people.
And what shall we do?
What can we do?

It is all a pity, you must be disappointed,
Go home and do something else for today,
Go home again, go home for today,
For you cannot hear the rabbit, under the earth,
Remarking rather sadly to himself, by himself,
As he rests in his warren, under the earth:
'It won't be long, they are bound to come,
They are bound to come and find me, even here!'

ALAN BROWNJOHN

The First Men on Mercury

– We come in peace from the third planet.
Would you take us to your leader?

– Bawr stretter! Bawr. Bawr. Stretterhawl?

– This is a little plastic model
of the solar system, with working parts.
You are here and we are there and we
are now here with you, is this clear?

– Gawl horrop. Bawr! Abawrhannahanna!

– Where we come from is blue and white
with brown, you see we call the brown
here 'land', the blue is 'sea', and the white
is 'clouds' over land and sea, we live
on the surface of the brown land,
all round is sea and clouds. We are 'men'.
Men come –

– Glawp men! Gawrbenner menko. Menhawl?

– Men come in peace from the third planet
which we call 'earth'. We are earthmen.
Take us earthmen to your leader.

– Thmen? Thmen? Bawr. Bawrhossop.
Yuleeda tan hanna. Harrabost yuleeda.

– I am the yuleeda. You see my hands,
we carry no benner, we come in peace.
The spaceways are all stretterhawn.

– Glawn peacemen all horrobhanna tantko!
Tan come at'mstrossop. Glawp yuleeda!

– Atoms are peacegawl in our harraban.
Menbat worrabost from tan hannahanna.

– You men we know bawrhossoptant. Bawr.
We know yuleeda. Go strawg backspetter quick.

– We cantantabawr, tantingko backspetter now!

– Banghapper now! Yes, third planet back.
Yuleeda will go back blue, white brown
nowhanna! There is no more talk.

– Gawl han fasthapper. . . ?

– No. You must go back to your planet.
Go back in peace, take what you have gained
but quickly.

– Stretterworra gawl, gawl . . .

– Of course, but nothing is ever the same,
now is it? You'll remember Mercury.

EDWIN MORGAN